COACHING YOUTH BASEBALL

How to Teach Pitching and Other Baseball Skills

David Grossman

editing & design
AnderssonPublishing.com

ISBN: 978-0-578-36056-0

Printed in the United States of America

Dedication

I'd like to dedicate this book to my family. My wife and best friend Dr. Mary Catherine McCabe learned how to keep score in 1999 so she could help me out on my very first team (and we weren't even married then). She loves games, so she adapted to baseball, but I know she would rather have been playing scrabble. Even now she always puts up with my coaching activities as she knows I love it, so she supports it. I am lucky to be married to her.

My two boys are the light of my life – Isaac is 17 and Joseph is 15 and both survived playing for me. They are both wonderful people and I will always be proud of them.

Our dog Bella, a four-year-old Goldendoodle, has been a source of much joy – what a great dog! – and she is now starting to learn how to catch.

PREFACE

It's said that it takes a village to raise a child. Generations ago, instead of two stressed-out working people trying to commute and raise kids, you had dozens of aunts, uncles, and grandparents to help out. With youth baseball, I think the same thing is true. Many teams have two assistants – but my teams typically have six or seven or even nine assistants. Everyone is on the field – parents, siblings, uncles, you name it – we use a village. And it's fun.

I decided I needed to write about it, as no one else does it – despite my advocating it when I was in charge of safety and training for my own league. Somewhere it seems to be written "And thou shalt have only two trusted assistants and thou shalt do thy best ... but good luck to you." Having just two assistants is probably fine when players are 15 or older. At that age they can do a ton of stuff on their own.

With kids ages 7 to 9 if you tell them "Go play catch" it's not going to go well. Sure, some can do it, but many of them can't. With everyone helping, though, you can put players in a position to succeed – you can generate positive reps and the kids get better quickly.

I have coached youth baseball for 25 seasons starting back in 1998. My intent here is to write a quick guide that will help new coaches.

First off, the key to a good practice is not two stations – it's SIX or SEVEN stations. But how do you set that up? In this book I'll show you how to make that happen, and I'll teach you the mechanics of what you do at each of the stations.

The book describes over 30 drills you can use to make practice fun and includes six detailed practice plans to cover early, mid, and late season practices for Tee Ball and kids pitch – and you should use a mix of these for coach pitch.

6 Key Points of the Book

1. Players don't keep playing if they aren't having fun – fun has to be included at every stage.

2. Players don't keep playing if they don't improve their skills. Always remember that and don't worry about the scoreboard as much as skill development. In professional baseball, the parent club rarely cares about the win/loss record of the minor league affiliates; they want skill development. Youth baseball should be all about skill development, too, and not just for the star players, but for everyone.

3. Some life lessons in baseball are taught more clearly than in other sports – it's a tough game that looks tantalizingly simple, but in reality it's not at all. Try hitting a rock thrown at you with everyone screaming advice and encouragement! Use this opportunity to teach kids life lessons.

4. Teaching the fundamentals of baseball, which require physical skills that involve muscle memory, does require countless reps. Some studies suggest 1900 reps are needed to nail down muscle memory – guitar players claim it's 30,000 and martial arts masters say it's 100,000. Point is, it's a lot! Be patient and maximize the quality repetitions by using the "whole village approach" – get as many parents involved as possible.

5. Your key measure of success should be player retention – if they keep playing you have done a great job. If you win all your games and no one wants to play anymore, you really haven't done a good job at all.

6. Focus on fundamentals at all times. Do not worry about turning the double play. Make the "simple" plays and very good things will happen. The little league team that makes every single "routine" play is very hard to beat. On offense, focus on just putting the ball in play; hitting home runs is nice, but just putting the ball in play puts a lot of pressure on the opposing defense.

INTRODUCTION

A typical youth team has one head coach and, if all goes well, one or two assistant coaches. These assistants are usually either friends of the head coach or parents who have said, "I'll be an assistant but don't have time to be a head coach." The head coach gets them together at the start of practice and says, "I'll work on the hitters, you do ground balls (to assistant #1) and (to assistant #2) you do fly balls." Done and Done. Three stations and off we go.

Some coaches have told me they were taught to fold a sheet of paper into quadrants and then put a station on each quadrant. That gives us FOUR stations – and that is TOO SMALL. What you actually need is seven or eight stations – or one station with seven or eight assistants at that station.

Why so many? Does that sound to you like chaos? You're thinking you'll never get that many assistants? "We only have an hour, by the time we set up seven stations practice will be over!"

Nope. You can do this. Here are the keys to making it work:

Early on, before you even begin the season, immediately ask all parents to help out, and explain why it matters to be an assistant coach. Tell them that we need a LOT of assistants. Parents are used to sports like soccer where they bring a child to the field and then sit in a chair and watch the practice while the coach runs around with the players. One of the differences between soccer and baseball is that one-on-ten actually works in soccer. Get a ball and play – the players will be entertained, they will get better at playing, and the coach will be fine.

Let's try it in basketball too – it actually works. Get a ball, drop it on the court and say PLAY, and bang – players will be happily running around on the court.

How about football? Yep, it works again – get a call and say PLAY and you're in business. Even in lacrosse – works there, too.

Now you see why the ten- or twelve-to-one ratio is firmly nailed into our youth sports culture. *It works in many sports.*

Now let's try baseball – one ball, one coach. Good so far. Now let's have these young kids go out in the field and let's pitch to one. Hmm, not quite as fun as we were thinking. First pitch: let's assume here that the coach is a great pitcher who can hit a 2-inch target (since our players are mighty small) and let's even make the leap here that the player hits the ball with no coaching on how to hit and that ball flies over to a player. What now? The fielder has no idea what to do with the ball. What are the other fielders doing? You've now got a fielder with an incoming ball and eight other kids with approximately nothing to do.

If we're lucky, they are all chasing the ball and happily participating in the practice game. Odds are, though, they are picking flowers, looking at an overhead airplane, watching a dog across the street – anything but even vaguely tracking the ball. In soccer the ball is nice and big and sitting on the ground. Kicking it does not require a big lesson in how to kick a ball; most kids can run up to a ball and kick it. With basketball it's a bit harder, but still most kids can pick up a ball and throw it, and maybe with a little work they can start dribbling. Nothing like baseball where everyone is staring at the sky or looking at bugs and then after a week or so of boredom, the parents say, "Oh, I guess baseball isn't for Johnny."

Recruit several assistants to help at every practice and good things will happen.

Is baseball not for Johnny or was practice so boring that it probably wasn't for anyone who was there?

Now imagine that we have seven or eight different stations – imagine that each station has one or two kids and an adult. Imagine that a specific skill is being taught. How much boredom is there now? Imagine that every two or three minutes someone yells SWITCH! and new things happen for every kid on the field. Orchestrating this is non-trivial, but it can be done. And the benefits are huge – instead of only a few kids who happen to have a good time on a baseball field with two stations, we now have the whole team liking baseball!

You might well ask what is so bad about three stations? Well, if you have a dozen players then you have four kids to a station. What is wrong with that? Well, if you have two assistant coaches, it's you and each assistant who get stations, and what is so bad about that? Well now we have a ratio of one adult to four players. Let's say you are working with the hitters – great, you now have four hitters trying to learn from you. How does that work? Let's say they are Bob, Sarah, Tommy, and Mary. "Okay Bob, come on over and hit some balls off the Tee, and Sarah, Tommy and Mary – YOU GO SIT DOWN AND WAIT YOUR TURN."

Sarah, Tommy, and Mary, if you are lucky, will sit quietly. If you are unlucky they will climb a fence, grab a big bat and start swinging it randomly. They'll get bored and grab a ball and play some catch. And what's so bad about that? Well, no one is watching them. Are they really learning anything? They're certainly not being coached, nor are they even practicing.

Let's move on to the other stations. At the ground ball station we have one assistant throwing balls out to four fielders. The throw happens, the player misses it, and the ball bounces 20 feet behind the player, who strolls back at a leisurely pace to get the ball and then throws it back over the coach's head. Congratulations, you now have had one repetition with just one of the four players. This is not what we call maximizing quality repetitions – which is actually the goal here. With numerous assistant coaches, three stations might be adequate. With a typical practice and only one assistant working with four players at a station, the practice cannot generate enough quality repetitions to teach the kids the skills they need to learn.

This book will show you how (and why) to set up and run six or seven or even eight stations with well-thought-out drills. You can set them all up and put yourself in the position of "RINGMASTER," where you walk around advising between stations, and make sure the transitions to different stations go quickly. You can teach things that need to be taught as you see them – you can work with all the players – but you are not actually running a station, because it's all delegated to the parents – your assistants. Of the 30+ drills provided here, you can use the ones that work best for your team.

AH HAH you say – *THAT'S THE CATCH – I can't get eight parents to agree to be assistants!* I can only get two! Now do you think that's because they don't want to do it? Did you really invite them? Trust me, you can indeed get at least four or five assistants, and four or five stations is way better than three. If you make it clear that the parents are desperately needed, they will help! This isn't soccer where you can roll one ball onto the field and say GO PLAY. The kids need to be taught very basic mechanics in baseball, and they need a LOT of reps.

You have one or two practices a week for youth baseball. You have to treat every minute as a gift from the heavens – and you need to maximize it.

The key is to have fun, keep learning, and remember that knowing how to play baseball has precious little to do with coaching it. Think of all the baseball hall-of-famers who got jobs as baseball managers. Some did well, but the vast majority simply struggled to articulate the steps beyond how they do something – the detailed pieces of hitting a triple or throwing from home to second base. Famous hitters are often interviewed about how to hit the ball and they say something like "I see it and then I hit it."

Whenever you learn a new skill, if you have success, that makes you want to keep learning it. If you don't have success you usually want to move on. I believe

This book will break down mechanics and give you some practice plans and fun drills to get the mechanics across.

every child can actually do just fine at Tee Ball and the parents who smile and say "Well, we learned that baseball wasn't really a good thing for our child" are really saying "Well, my child had a coach who really didn't engage the players and ensure they developed their skills." Retention rates in Tee Ball are really bad – just *hoping* that players will play even if their skills do not develop is really a big stretch. Your job is to improve their skills and to do it in a fun way – because ultimately you want every last one of your kids to play again next season.

Despite all the fine YouTube videos out there (some by us) and a few other very good books, we just didn't see the emphasis on retention, on parent involvement at practice, and on skill development that really must be present. This book covers the hows and whys of all those, particularly the very strong focus you need on kids' skill development.

We start out with communication with your team, drills for basic skills needed for youth baseball throwing, ground balls and hitting – and then we provide practice plans along with a few real-world stories so you can learn what to expect.

Have fun and let us know how it goes!

Coach David Grossman
January 2022

COMMUNICATING WITH THE TEAM

The First Parent Letter

When you have your team roster, send them all a short email to let them know you are the coach and when you'll be practicing. Tell them that it's critical that at least one parent per player comes dressed and ready to help at each practice. Tell them they are all assistant coaches – and the only way to achieve the skill development players need is if the parents come out and help.

Think about it: No parent of a 5-year-old is going to just drop them off at the field and go run errands. They are going to stay – so why not wear some tennis shoes and help out? Parents (i.e. assistant coaches) don't need baseball expertise. Here's an example email (one that we used last year in the spring):

> Welcome to the Junior Cactus League. My name is David Grossman and I am the manager – with strong help from the assistant managers John Smith, Kathy Jones, Sally Patrick, Paul Marks, and Chris Johnson.
> First and foremost, my goal is to do all I can so your child learns so much and has so much fun that they want to play next year.
> Your player does need a glove; if you don't have one, you can buy a used one from Charley's Sports. Any comfortable shoes – sneakers or rubber cleats – are fine. Uniforms including shirts, hats, pants, and socks will be provided. Your child may bring their own bat and helmet, or they can use the team bats and helmets. If you really want to get your child their own bat, please talk to me about it so it'll be the right size. Practices – Our practices are scheduled at MidCity Field on Thursdays. It'll just be an hour and I want to pick a time that works for the most people, because my teams always rely on extensive parent participation at practice. I know this is not easy with traffic and other issues, but if we can get a bunch of parents to

help, it'll make an enormous difference. We really need to maximize quality repetitions. A typical Tee Ball practice looks like one coach rolling balls to a few players, another coach tossing balls, and another working on hitting. Imagine instead that every player has an adult rolling them a ball in a line – instead of taking turns and waiting on the coach to get to the players, we get LOTS more reps for all the kids.

And it's fun for the parents too!

Practices will be a max of 1 hour – and please remember to provide your player with water. Please respond to this email if you will be able to assist during practices, and let me know the hour that works best for you, e.g. 5:30 to 6:30 or 6:00 to 7:00.

Games – we will play on Saturdays. I ask that your player be at the field and ready to play 30 minutes prior to the start of each game. We will run a warmup that really depends on everyone being there. Let me know if you have any questions; you can email me at <email> or call my cell at <number>.

Thanks and I can't wait to meet everyone. I'll add the practices to the calendar, and I'll fill in the time once I get some responses.

The First Parent Meeting

This is a big moment in coaching a Tee Ball season. You need LOTS of parents to help – they may have older kids who did Tee Ball with a team that had just one, two, or maybe three coaches who ran everything, and the parents gave the coaches a gift certificate at the end of the season, and HEY, those kids turned out fine, and so they are expecting to not have to be really involved.

This is your chance to change things.

Just because a youth practice *can* be run by four adults doesn't mean that it's a good idea. In fact it's a VERY BAD idea. But then why does it work? It works just because kids are happy to do nothing but be outside, so if that's all they're doing they won't mutiny on you. If they have to wait at the end of a big line to get ground balls, they will wait. It's not clear that their skills will be sacrificed much if they miss a few reps, so why not? On the other hand, it's really a missed opportunity.

I ran a Tee Ball team a few years ago and the team stayed with me for the first season of machine pitch. The second season we played machine pitch again. There was no official score kept but the league decided the team must not play together ever again and it must be split apart. Why? Because we executed very simple plays. A ground ball to the pitcher was an out. A ground ball to second base was an out. On offense everyone swung the bat and put the ball in play. Nothing fancy, but the league said that it was unfair that not all players got the "benefit of our coaching."

Parents and other coaches just do not like to lose.

The real reason is that parents and other coaches do not like to lose and by any account they weren't just losing, they were losing by wide margins. I heard other parents lament about the bad luck that such fantastic players all got put on the same team. Note that there was no draft and I promise I did no recruiting. In my mind I had already coached all-star teams (I got into coaching before I had kids) and now I was going to just have fun with my oldest son. I was not trying to take the fun out of it for the league. I simply told the parents that I thought we needed LOTS of assistants, I got a bunch of them, and quite honestly not everything came together right away. But by our third season, call it a year's time, the basics were being executed where other teams were just not anywhere close.

So do I think the approach laid out here is some magic bullet that will guarantee that all players will play professionally and obtain college scholarships? No I don't. However, I did track that team and no one quit baseball for three seasons, which is unheard of at that level.

Traditionally, players play and then if it doesn't go well for them they quit and their parents say "Oh well, baseball is not for them." I just don't believe it – I think with enough quality repetitions and fun in practice, everyone can stick around long enough for baseball to become really fun. By the way, I was heartbroken when they split up my team and I argued that it wasn't my fault that other coaches wouldn't do the same thing I was doing, but alas, the league was firm and we were split up. Happily five members of that team have gone on to play baseball and they all still keep in touch. You might just surmise that it was just luck that I had such good players, but believe me, there were plenty of players on that team that lacked natural athletic talent and I don't think they would be upset to read this (or at least I hope not).

This past year, I was an assistant on a AA (ages 7-9 in Little League) team. The team went 12-1 in a league that was well balanced. More important, every player says they want to play next year (okay, one seems on the fence but I am pretty sure he will play).

There was no draft, so one can argue that we just lucked into unbelievable players. There is some truth but I really think our "whole village" approach was the difference. I volunteered to work with the pitchers and the head coach took my advice to invite lots of assistants.

During a typical practice, we had a batting practice (coach pitch) station in the infield, a hitting station with whiffle balls over in left field (with three coaches either doing soft toss or pitching whiffle balls to swiftsticks), a kid pitch station in center field to work on pitching mechanics, and a ground ball station in right field. The kid pitch station had two coaches, the left field station had three coaches, the center field station had at least one coach, and the right field station had a least one coach. To do this requires a minimum of four coaches, and doing it well takes five or six. Most teams have just three; at some practices we had as many as eight. I attribute the success of the team to the "whole village" approach where lots of assistant coaches were deployed to maximize reps. Many of the parents / assistants told me they loved how our practices were action-packed and they enjoyed helping rather than just sitting on the sideline watching kids. They also liked how we always focused on mechanics, and we spent effort and time on fixing bad mechanics vs just "playing a scrimmage." I'll be the first to admit we had some great players, but I very much attribute the team success to our highly energized practices.

Getting a field reserved, putting together a team, getting kids to practice – these are little things that are precious – why not use the time wisely and efficiently? Why just have parents sitting on the sideline watching or checking their phones

Your agenda for the initial parents' meeting really has only one key point: We want to maximize quality reps so the kids get better and keep playing.

when they could be helping you and the kids maximize reps, build skills, and get good at baseball?

Explain to them that your goal is that all the kids play again next season. That should be it. Just imagine if you put the same kid in the pitcher spot for the entire Tee Ball season. How is that going to help the kids who never get to be in the pitcher spot? Will they be excited about playing again? NO THEY WON'T.

Tell the parents that we will try to *gamify* drills (turn them into fun games) to increase fun for the kids, and we will use *peer modeling* so they can "coach" other kids and identify areas for improvement. Get it across to the parents that in Tee Ball of all places, you will ROTATE the positions – like it's done in volleyball. *Everyone plays everywhere equally.* You're going to be teaching a few skills. There is no need to deploy complex strategy in Tee Ball or coach pitch – if your league is any good, no score will be kept in these young age level games. We just want to get kids to play everywhere. Keeping Tee Ball score is bad, because it puts coaches in a position where they feel obligated to go out there and try to win. In major league baseball, minor league coaches are not evaluated by the number of games they win – instead they are evaluated by *how well they develop players.* Too often a coach who loses games is just not a great coach. We *say* it's all about development, but a coach who loses all his games tends to be viewed in a negative light. Coaches know this at the younger levels, so they stop developing players – instead of maybe putting a kid who can't really catch at first base, they put the one kid who *can* catch at first. They say "BUT I HAD TO DO IT – that kid was the only one who could catch."

No, they didn't have to do it; the scoreboard inspired them to do it. Instead, *teach them all to catch and play them all at first!* You never know what might happen. If kids know they are going to be counted on to make some plays, well, they'll work pretty hard at making the plays. I haven't met a kid yet who wants to let their team down.

> Tell parents that the skills we need to teach are:
> A. How to throw to a target
> B. How to field a ground ball and then throw to a target
> C. How to hit a ball
> D. How to run the bases – in the correct order and in a straight line
> E. How to catch a fly ball
> F. How to catch a ball that's thrown to you
> G. A little bit on getting players started with pitching

We will provide detailed drills and photos for each of these skills. Explain to the parents that E and F just can't always happen for some Tee Ball players, so those two skills will get less emphasis. Many players age 5 or 6 just can't do some advanced physical skills like catching a fly ball – it's hard at that age. You have to judge where the ball is, where it will be, how fast it's going and how to get your glove there at the same time. That level of physical coordination often does not develop until age 7 or 8 – so for us it won't be a key point of practice. There is so much else to do.

To do these skills the team will be running drills, and kids need REPS and FEEDBACK, and to maximize this we need a ton of coaches. Our best and most effective team practices had one adult for each child. Compare that to just three coaches on the field. Imagine how much more engaged the kids will be if they are surrounded by adults and the adults are motivated to maximize reps.

For the next part of your meeting tell them that SNACK must happen after every game, and for many Tee Ball kids, SNACK is a highlight. So make it a good one and make sure the whole team eats their snack together. For your parents' meeting hour, take 2 minutes on snack and 58 minutes on why you need everyone's help at practice.

Walk the parents through the following scenario – ground ball drill. Each parent rolls a ball to a child and the child throws it back. As you can imagine, the throws are pretty wild. If we have only a few parents helping – and photo that – they have to go get the ball and bring it back, or the child has to go get it behind them if they miss the ground ball. Every second that kids are casually strolling over to pick up a ground ball is a second wasted – a rep wasted. You want to have lots of balls on hand to make sure that when balls are missed, they can leave them alone. It's all to maximize reps. *Quality repetitions are the key to kids' learning* in baseball, especially at this young age. As they learn what it feels like to do each skill, they repeat that feeling, that skill, till they become familiar with it.

ESTABLISH THE CLASSROOM

Before we get started on skill development, we need to discuss the establishment of your classroom. You are coaching, yes, but you are also teaching. Coaching implies you determine the batting lineup, work things out with the umpire, deal with the parents, help out with the league fundraiser, and numerous other responsibilities, but most important is that *you are teaching baseball.* And if you are to teach you have to have a classroom setting with actual discipline and organization.

Take a good look at this image. I see countless coaches start talking to players and the players aren't even looking at them. Suppose you are saying something like, "Please call for a fly ball before you catch it." Well that's an important thing to teach. If the players have never heard you say that, then how to you expect them to do it?

That's me in the photo with some kids and I'm about to teach them something. Notice they are on one knee, so they aren't wandering around. Notice that their eyes are locked on me or I won't start talking. Notice their hands are on their knees so they won't pick at the grass and throw it at each other. This takes practice and it's important to nail down. Notice I'm on one knee myself so I am close to eye level and this enables me to talk TO them and not AT them. I am NOT wearing sunglasses when I address the players – they need to see me. They need to be able to read my body language and know that I mean what I say and I will always be honest and I have respect for them. Young people do not have large vocabularies, but they are very adept at reading body language. Make it easy for them.

I have a thing I do at the first practice which is that I show my kids how to be on one knee. I show them how to not bump into each other and how to not pick grass. Then I have them stand up, and I move over to another spot and count down 5-4-3-2-1 and then they are on one knee. Notice that being on one knee means your classroom is good for about 60 seconds at a time. No one needs a three-hour lecture at a 60-90 minute practice.

Think about what you are going to say and get it across quickly and succinctly. Just pretend you are giving a TED Talk and you only have one minute.

Use simple words, and if you use a long word, ask them if they know it. I used the word "sequence" one day and I asked if anyone knew what it was, and most of them said no. So don't assume everyone knows big words that get taught in high school. I usually call the team together at the start of practice, at the end, and before key sequences begin in practice. I always try to keep it to one minute and if possible 30-45 seconds. Two minutes is an absolute maximum.

Also do not get distracted. Many times a player will raise a hand impatiently and really look like they have a critical item for discussion. I always call on them and say BE QUICK. Then they ask, "What is the snack plan for after practice?" and I ask, "How is that related to what I was talking about?!" Tell them practice is only for a short time, so you really need them to stay focused.

Make sure you are clear that everyone needs to stay on topic. Be consistent, do this all the time, and after a while the team will just lock into it. Note this can be done for Tee ball – it is harder at that age but it can be done. For coach pitch, it absolutely can be done and after that it's not even all that hard. I will say for 12-13 year olds I have them just stand and circle around me as I want to talk to them for longer periods of time. We can't really have a big conversation about how to take a lead off a left-handed pitcher vs a right-handed pitcher in 30 seconds. It's very valuable with the younger kids to teach them to hold still and focus.

SKILL DEVELOPMENT

Now that you have your team and have talked with the parents, it's time to cover the key points in skill development for Tee Ball. Throwing to a target is the most important. If players start to learn to throw and do it accurately, they can see how they can help their team. Hitting is of course important – and what person doesn't want to grab a bat and hit a home run with it? There's something intrinsically fun about hitting a ball – so you as a coach can leverage that to make practice fun by doing plenty of hitting.

Catching a thrown ball is not always all that doable in Tee Ball – a few kids can manage it, but many childhood development books suggest that tracking a flying ball is a skill that often does not develop until a child is 7 or 8 years old. Some of the kids will be able to catch, but you shouldn't make it a central thing to teach your players.

Finally there is basic knowledge of baseball – do not assume that your players know which way to run the bases, let alone where all the positions actually are.

"It turns out that baseball is just not for Johnny."

In this book are some practice plans that use these skills, and you'll be off and running. Skill development is critical to player retention, but there is no cookie cutter plan for this. You will have to be tougher on the kids who are getting the hang of it and at the same time be a little nicer to the kids who aren't.

Always remember that kids develop at different rates – but that EVERYONE can do these skills.

We hate it when we hear, "Oh, this kid isn't cut out for baseball." Sure he is. But this happens to kids whose athletic or mental or physical development is a bit slower than the other kids. So this kid often ends up getting less coaching, receives less care and feeding, and then chooses not to play again – and everyone is happy.

"Oh, we tried it and baseball's just not for Johnny." That's just great – that kid unfortunately misses out on some of the great life lessons that baseball offers – how to overcome failure (it's not easy to publicly hit a ball thrown toward you from a distance) and how to be part of a team and how to communicate with teammates. Do whatever you can to not let this happen to any of your kids!

Baseball is a game of failure – and learning to fail and recover and get back up again is a valuable life lesson. It is hard to teach this in other sports where failure doesn't occur as frequently or as clearly. It's easy to blame someone else for a missed score in soccer or basketball or football, but when you strike out, it was just you and the pitcher.

SKILL A: THROW TO A TARGET

Drill: Basic throwing is the precursor to pitching

Throwing to a target is hard. Throwing accurately every time is much harder, and throwing with velocity from a distance with accuracy is even harder.

The best players in the world make some bad throws. If you watch a youth game with 11-12 year old players you'll often see that the cause of most errors is erratic throws. A throw that pulls the first baseman off the bag by one step is enough to make a team lose a game. We focus on only routine throws.

The bullet throw from the knees is not a thing you need to care about in youth baseball – the kids will grow up soon enough. Get the routine throws down, and very good things will happen for your kids. Also, teaching throwing at a young age sets the stage to teach pitching when the kids reach an age where they are playing kid-pitch ball (usually age 9 or 10). If you can't throw accurately you are never going to pitch accurately. The kids who pitch almost always stay with baseball, as the game ends up being about 90 percent pitching. A team that throws strikes consistently with several pitchers has a huge advantage.

So how to teach throwing to a kid who can barely pick up a ball? It's not easy. The ball doesn't fit in their little hands, and worse for the teacher/coach, throwing to a specific target is just NOT FUN. Throwing as far as you can in whatever direction is actually a blast for small kids. They just love to do it. So now with the inclusion of a target, you are trying to do something that is less fun for them.

Let's try to teach just one kid to throw, and then we will talk about how to get a team to do it. There are several things you need to get started ...

If possible, draw a line on the ground between the kid and the target. A parking lot with chalk lines is great, but that doesn't often make itself available on a practice field. You can, however, lay down a rope between the thrower and the target. A rope works well, pink flagging works well, or you can just tell the player to imagine a nice line.

Now you need a bucket of balls – you don't want to kill a half hour chasing erratic throws. Once the kids have thrown a bucket of balls – 20 or 30 of them – that's probably as many reps as you can hope for in a day and that's typically about 10-15 minutes. If you get kids to throw 10-15 minutes a day, even just once a week, you'll see improvement soon and considerable improvement by the end of the season. If you can get parents to work with the kids 2-3 days a week, you'll see decent improvement after about a month. If you get them to do it every day you'll see the improvement in just 2-3 weeks. Remember these are just averages and your mileage may vary.

For this first drill, no glove is used. First you must decide which handed the player is. Just drop some balls on the ground, have them pick up the balls and throw them, and you'll see which hand they use. Go with that one.

Just to keep this simple, we will describe all of this for a RIGHT-HANDED player who will be throwing with the right hand. Just reverse the feet and hands for left-handed kids.

Step 1: Have the player pick up a ball and hold it, not too tightly but not too loosely.

Step 2: Put both hands together at the chest level; feet are slightly wider than hip width apart. This is a big deal because it puts the player into a POWER POSITION – think middle linebacker in football – eyes focused on the target.

Weight is on the balls of the feet, with hands slightly away from the chest. *Watch carefully for bad habits* like putting the feet too close together, or putting the ball against the chest. Knees have to be flexed just a little – watch that they don't crouch down with knees bent or stand too tall with knees straight.

A bad habit for many young players is starting with the knees locked; *it's much easier to fix this when they are 5* than it is when they are 10 years old after 5 years of doing it.

The feet have to be at the right width. These three photos show the stance too narrow, feet just right, and feet too wide. You will know the feet are correctly placed when you can lightly push the player's chest and they won't fall backward. The feet at shoulder width apart with knees slightly bent and weight slightly forward is a fundamental athletic posture in many sports, and it applies in baseball when throwing, catching, and hitting.

Step 3: Have the player point the left arm to the target and SAY "AIMER."

Non-throwing arm is straight pointed to the target, fingers extended. Knees are slightly bent. Key teaching point here is that the ball is pointed AWAY from the target. The throwing elbow is lightly bent and the elbow is above the shoulder. Note in this photo the player is holding a tennis ball, but it doesn't matter. I use tennis balls a lot at the start of season until I know the players can catch. Making the leap from a tennis ball to a baseball is not a big deal, and you don't want to start off the season with kids getting hurt and generating a fear of the ball.

Before going on to Step 4, have each player do Steps 1, 2 and 3 a few times. **Never add a step until the previous steps are looking good.**

Point the left arm straight at the target and say AIMER, with the ball pointed AWAY from the target. Use tennis balls when you start this exercise.

The key is that the ball must be pointing away.

← If the ball is facing the target, the arm motion will change when the throw reaches this point and begins to push the ball rather than PULL the ball – and pulling is what we want. Notice the ball here is NOT pointed away from the target. This is easy to correct at a young age; it's much harder when they are 12 years old.

Step 4: Now the right hand goes back like pulling on a slingshot, such that the ball points away from the target.

Back when two fingers meant a "Peace sign" we would say *Peace sign to center field.* We clearly need new cues for this one; you can teach kids the Peace sign or "V for Victory" or you can just say ARM BACK and then correct it and they'll get it.

So now your checkpoints are:

- Ball pointed away from target
- Elbow lightly bent
- Elbow above shoulder
- Feet shoulder width apart
- Weight on balls of feet

Step 5: This photo shows a stride and the whole body right on a line with the target. As you progress you can gradually merge steps 4 and 5 and just say "Stride and Arm Back."

The next photo shows the toes stepping off to the player's left. This now forces the player to throw-push the ball and not generate any power from the lower body. This is super common and it's very hard to fix. One good way to fix it is to use a rope and have the player step on the line with the rope and then step back. Film study helps too – show the player that they are doing it. Showing them in front of a mirror helps. Most players who do this don't even notice they are doing it, and fixing it for them will make a huge difference in power and accuracy.

When the toes step too far to the player's left, he has to push the ball, making it hard to generate power from the lower body.

Step 6: THROW – finally the throwing arm moves and releases the ball. Tell the player to hold the ball longer than they might think to and then follow through. The arm is going at high speed, and if the arm stops right at the throw then that means it slowed down during the throw, or the kid slowed the arm right after the throw. This puts a lot of stress on the arm and is a bad habit you should spot and break right now.

Here's a player with a good step and the back foot turned, ready to throw. The hips are engaged, but the shoulders are bunched up close to the ears, making him look less comfortable and making it harder for him to throw. Players sometimes get tense before a throw; it's important for them to relax or "drop" their shoulders for the entire drill.

Here's how you drill this with more than one player. Start with the players about 10 feet apart, and if they are throwing more or less accurately, move them a few feet back. Distance magnifies error, so they can do everything wrong when they're close and still throw accurately. Kids who can do this will cause much pain to the coach for trying to teach the right thing; there's not much worse than a parent whose kid is just strong and does it all wrong and the parent hits you with WHY ARE YOU "FIXING" MY KID?

If they're doing it incorrectly but more or less accurately, have them throw from farther away and see if the accuracy is still there – usually it isn't. If a kid is throwing perfectly, have the parent across from them move the target around – high above their head sometimes, low sometimes, you get the idea.

For a full team drill you need two lines, one with kids throwing and one with parents catching. They are spaced far apart (at least 10 feet between each of the parents) so that bad throws from one kid will not kill another parent.

Each player should have four or five balls next to them. Act like it's a rifle range and call out the steps: FEET WIDE, HANDS TOGETHER, AIMER, ARM BACK, STRIDE TOWARD THE TARGET, THROW. Correct things you see at each step. Coaches should be about 15-20 feet apart for Tee ball and around 30-35 feet apart for 8-9 year olds in coach pitch.

As you start working with pitchers you want to make sure the distance is 46 feet. The best way to do this is to cut a rope and put a knot in it at the 46-feet mark and lay it out so you know you have the measurement correct.

Tell them the first thrower to ten points gets a prize – do anything you can think of to keep them interested – because in real life this is a boring drill. There's no way to make it super fun (at least not one I have found). Some parents have told me that you could make it fun by having the kids breathe some helium and do squeaky voices, but I'm not a proponent of that approach.

Even boring skills drills can be great fun if you turn it into a competition.

One way to make it fun is to turn it into a fierce competition. Johnny has 5 points and Paul has 3 – c'mon Paul, you don't want to have fewer points do you?? The prize for the drill can be the lamest of things, really, kids this age don't care. They just like to get points and win prizes. The prize can even be the first kid who gets to hit off the Tee or whatever!

There are lots of variations for this drill for older kids, but alas for Tee Ball, this drill is the nuts and bolts. Get this working and eventually you can skip the steps – you can just say pick up a ball and throw and it'll work. Use the steps, though, until everything looks good.

Some of this is actually muscle memory. If a kid has been throwing with the wrong mechanics, he now has to unlearn some stuff, and this is far easier to do when the kid is 5 years old. Remember, muscle memory takes NINE HUNDRED REPS to change. So in 15 minutes we are going to get, if we are lucky, about 20 throws in. We need to do this drill 40 times to get to 800 reps.

Now you see why we are into maximizing reps by maximizing parents who help coach. If we have only 10 practices a season, you might think we get only 200 reps, but we also have about 10 *games* a season, and guess what – we can do this BEFORE EVERY GAME – it's called warming up.

So we can get to 400 reps without doing anything special, and if a kid works with a parent one or two extra days a week then we can fairly easily get to the target 900 reps we need.

Remember that kids at this age develop physically at different rates – and mentally too. Some days you've done really well if you can get them to just pay attention instead of watching birds and airplanes.

Drill: Two knees, isolate the upper body

After a while if players are kind of getting the hang of Throwing Drill #1 you can introduce a progression of throwing. The progression starts with two knees throwing. You can place five balls beside each player and tell them to do this for five throws and then move on to the next drill. This avoids the need to go chase balls. Feel free to substitute tennis balls as not everyone has accumulated a zillion balls from coaching for a long time.

This one is harder for kids, but it's a good one to add some variety, and as the season progresses it's good for the kids and for the team to do different things. This drill isolates the arms; you just face the target – bellybutton toward the target, say AIMER, bring the lead arm to the target, arm up, and they pick up a ball and bend their elbow, say ARM BACK (this is just to bring the elbow above the shoulder), and then throw.

Let's take it slowly. First we start with hands together. Note that we are facing the target head-on as this happens after the hips turn in a throw. We are really starting at the end of the throw. By isolating the upper body there are fewer things that go wrong. Let's take it step by step.

Step 1: Hands together, look at the target

Sometimes it's good to point out what not to do. The next photo I asked the players to all look down at the ground and then up at the sky. They had fun with this but it shows them the eyes must be locked on the target.

Step 2: Aim and Arm Up

Now we are going to aim at the target and bring our arm up so that elbow is above shoulder. We are not going to use our hips (that's for the next drill). The really big moment in this whole drill is to get the elbow above the shoulder and this is the step where you can focus on it. I find with new players they really have to build up some strength in their arms and shoulder before they can actually keep the elbow above shoulder for more than a second or two. But that strength will come if you keep practicing this one.

Step 3: Squeeze the fist of the lead arm.

I like this one as it's building a strong front side. We don't want the lead arm to go flying around. I find if they squeeze their fist it's less likely to move around. This is a precursor to some pitching drills that start with the player squeezing their glove before they launch. (Note I usually skip this step and Step 4 in Tee Ball but introduce them in coach pitch.

Step 4: Turn the lead arm and bend the elbow.

This is all part of a strong front side and is a precursor to pitching drills. Again, you can skip steps 3 and 4 here if you are not comfortable with them or if you are coaching Tee Ball, but I find them helpful even though it's not as important as keeping eyes on the target and the elbow above the shoulder.

Step 5: Throw

Now they throw the ball, and you ask them to bend their back at the same time. We are trying to instill the notion that bending at the waist will add power to the throw. Also the throwing arm should travel across the body. Sometimes I put something on the ground and have them pick it up so they get the notion that the arm goes across the body. This helps them learn to not slow down their arm during the throw. Sometimes I sit in front of them and have them slap my hand with their throwing arm so they know to continue the throw.

This simulates the action after the stride and right at the release of the throw. Sometimes kids really benefit from this one, because it's obvious if they are dropping their elbow below their shoulder. Many kids need to develop some arm strength to keep that elbow above the shoulder – and this drill will help with that.

There are two good variations of the two-knee drill. One is to just bring the throwing arm to a position where the elbow is above the shoulder and then throw.

The second is to cock the hips and bring the arm all the way back and then throw. The first ensures that the elbow is above the shoulder without involving the hips, and the second involves the hips. Doing these in a sequence is a good thing if you have the time.

Drill: Standing — No Hips — No Stride

Now we gradually introduce the lower body. Standing up includes the knees, but we'll wait on the stride and the use of the hips. This goes quickly because your players have done this on two knees – feet wide, aim, and arm back. Make sure eyes are on the target, with the elbow above the shoulder. The photos show eyes on the target, eyes looking at the ground or up in the sky; be sure to add some fun into every practice.

Next: Squeeze – same as before, but squeeze the lead hand into a fist:

Turn – Same as before, but turn the arm and bend the elbow:

In the next step, have them throw and bend their backs when they throw.

Now just have the kids throw for a while – and notice that three players in the photo above bent their backs and two of them didn't! This shows examples of both right and wrong in one photo.

Most young pitchers do not bend their backs and I suspect that this is a root cause of numerous arm problems later on – *please teach your kids about this* early in life. Get them to use the whole body to throw, not just the arm.

Drill: Standing Up — Add Hips

Now we have the players stand up, thus no longer isolating the lower body. The key thing is that we want them to feel their hips. To emphasize the hips, have them just put their feet forward, keep them there, and just cock their hips.

Here you can see a line of players where they have stood up and come to ready position, and then I said **Ready** (they put their hands together), **Aim** (and they aim their lead hand to the target and focus on the target), and **Turn hips** (and with this cue, the players' feet stay forward and they just turn their hips).

Some players' left knees will bend when they are turning their hips. Just check and make sure the elbow is above the shoulder, with good extension.

Then tell them **Throw**, and they release their hips and throw the ball. This usually feels pretty good, and many players will see right away that the ball goes much farther and faster than if they do not cock their hips. You can have them try it with and without the hips to get the feel of it.

Players usually really enjoy this one as they see the ball flying and they never even had to stride. You can emphasize that once the stride becomes a part of this, very good things will happen. Have them practice this drill for a while, and be sure you assist any players who are confused or just don't get it. Go back to the previous drill if you think it will help them, and remember that you will have some kids who just aren't coordinated or developed enough at this level to do this consistently. Individual encouragement, and showing them how, can be really useful with learning this.

Drill: Put it together — stand up, add the stride

Now we are ready for the whole thing, including both upper body and lower body working together.

Stand with the throwing shoulder facing target, feet wide, knees bent. Say *"aimer and arm back"* and have them point the throwing arm at the target and bring the arm back.

Next, Step and throw. Remember to watch for bending the back. Have the player step toward the target while the arm is going back.

The arm gets to the farthest point from the target at the same time the lead foot lands. The hips fire, and the back foot turns, and the arm continues to the opposite side of the body – *and the back bends.* I strongly suggest you have each player freeze at the end of the throw, so you can see if they bent their back – and whether their eyes are on the target.

It will help if you have them step toward the target, then bring the stepping foot back, then step again and throw. This "practice step" sort of gets it into their head that there will be a good step toward the target. It's easy to remove the practice step once they get the hang of how this works. Once you have done all the throwing drills then you can boil it down to these four points:

1.   Ready Position, hands together and ready to throw.

2.   Stride and Arm Back – have the player step toward the target and bring the arm back. Make sure the eyes are on the target and the throwing

elbow is above the shoulder with good extension. The ball is pretty far away from the player, so the player can use the whole arm for the throw. This really does work if you do this repeatedly over time, with patience. You will see amazing progress. To start with I say *STRIDE AND ARM BACK* to cue this one.

3.   Now Squeeze the Glove – turn the glove toward the face and turn the back foot at the same time. I usually say *SQUEEZE AND TURN* to cue this one.

If a player gets to this position, the throw is going to be straight. The whole body is in line, and the launch point is in a perfect position.

What we are doing here is *teaching the body what it feels like* to get into a very good position to throw. This helps throwing and this helps pitching, but it does take time. Players may feel a little awkward at first, but you're teaching them how it feels and they'll improve with repetition!

Next say *THROW.*

Notice how the ball is launched nicely and is going straight. Notice how the player's head is facing the target and everything is in line.

This throw actually went over my head, and I was a good 25 feet away from my nephew. Many players on this year's team started the season throwing the ball far, but they had no idea where the ball was going. I emphasized that we needed to have a consistent throwing motion so the ball would go straight to the target. I did not correct everything or try to turn them into little robots who threw exactly the same way – everyone is different, and every player has a different body composition. However, a few things are common in all good pitchers / throwers. The keys are that they always step in line with the target –

41

and that is why the stride toward the target is the first step. They also always have their elbow above their shoulder so they get good extension.

When working with young players, don't try to correct 50 things at once. Let them throw a couple of times with no correction just to start to get comfortable in the environment for the day. Then start with one problem and work on fixing it. Usually fixing one key thing during a practice is plenty. Next practice, you can work on the next thing."

Get each player to focus on one thing at a time, even if you can see 4 things they need to work on. Once they do it right, have them repeat it – a lot.

If the player constantly drops the elbow below the shoulder, keep pointing it out and correcting it; try to get the player some good quality reps. Making too many corrections all at once will just confuse the player. For most kids, the key is to get their elbow above the shoulder with good extension and a good stride – and then very good things will happen.

Once they learn to do this in drills, try to put them in situations where they might naturally revert to their old form, and then correct it. The key is to get them to where this becomes muscle memory and it happens all the time and not just during a drill. Remember that muscle memory takes time, so be patient and be consistent.

SKILL B: FIELDING
A GROUND BALL

Before starting any drills, I have the kids really *focus on getting to the ready position*. I recommend getting the players to say CREEP-CREEP-SHOW where they step forward with very very small steps with one foot and then the other, and then <u>show</u> their glove. This sort of gets them moving and on the balls of their feet, and they're ready to go left or right.

"Showing the glove" means to turn the glove so that it's ready to come down to the ground (see the glove nicely open and ready to receive the ball). I try to teach players to do this whenever the pitcher lifts up the front leg to begin the pitch. It takes a lot of repetitions to make this a habit, but it will pay big dividends if you teach it and make it happen.

Most missed ground balls aren't because of mechanics, but more that the player is a little surprised the ball is coming to them. If they creep and show, they are often in a great position to move right to the ball.

Finally, have players shuffle their feet side to side to get a feel for moving laterally to the ball without crossing their legs.

Drill: Attack a Standing Ball

This one is easy, and it teaches the ready position. Step one is feet wide, knees bent, and glove at hip level.

Have the player run toward a cone (which you have placed about 10 feet in front of them) and "land the airplane" as the glove comes down to the ground. This teaches attacking ground balls and gradually lowering the glove (good) versus running to the ball and squatting over it (not good), which is what kids often do.

You just need a ball on the ground and your players can work on their approach. As they get better tell them CREEP-CREEP-SHOW and have them take a small step with the left foot, a small step with the right foot, and then *show their open glove* at hip level.

Knees bent, weight on the balls of the feet ... then say GO and have them move toward the ball.

Here we have a player who has the legs straight and the head down instead of looking toward the ball. The key is to *lower the body by bending the knees* while still keeping the arms extended.

Here we have a player whose legs are crossed, not at all ready to get the ball.

Many pitchers at this level have trouble throwing strikes, so players will naturally lose focus. Crossed legs like this is very common and a tip-off that you should watch out for.

This player is not bending the knees and the feet are too wide to be in a good ready position.

Drill: Attack a Ball Rolled to You

With this drill you will roll a ball in their general direction and have them run up and get it into their glove, thus catching a ground ball. Have the assistant coaching parents roll balls slowly. Parents should be on their knees, and the balls should be easy. No hard hops, no backhands, nothing difficult and nothing fancy.

We are focusing on the routine here. If they get it happily, you can then get some throwing work in, as they now can field a ground ball and then go through the steps of throwing, making for more reps for throwing while you're teaching ground balls!

Drill: Fielding grounders, throwing to a target

Now we will set up a target and roll the ball to the player – and as you roll it, you start counting. Most youth baseball players can run from home to first in about four seconds, so I like to *count down loudly 4-3-2-1* as I roll the ball toward the fielder. This helps them strike a balance between rushing (and being out of control) and simply waiting for the ball to eventually get to them.

This player is READY to field a ground ball!

The idea is to charge and attack the ball, cover it like an alligator, bring the ball toward the body, and then set the feet and throw to the target. Most players easily get the idea of setting their feet instead of throwing on the run. If the player has trouble throwing it a long distance, it's fine for them to shuffle and then throw. If the ball gets back to you when you are on 4 or 3, they are probably going too fast and not setting their feet. If the ball gets back to you at 2 or even at 1 it's usually a pretty good play. Players will self-correct if you keep doing this, and it can be done with several coaches rolling balls to players. The more reps you can do on this the more it becomes muscle memory or a habit for young players.

To make it more fun I put coaches on the infield grass with the players lined up at first base, and then go to the first base position. The coach will then hold

the ball up, wait for the player to say and do the "creep-creep-show" and then roll the ball and start counting down from 4-1.

The player will attack the ball, cover it like an alligator, come up and set their feet and throw to the coach.

Once they are done, they move to second base position, where a coach is waiting to roll the ball from the infield grass. Next they can move to shortstop, and finally to third base, where they can run behind home and get back in line at first base.

This has the advantage of giving each player four repetitions quickly, and then a little break. Also while in line they can watch players who are fielding. It is often good to have one player stand next to the coaches and help "coach" players – when they see mistakes – or the right way to do it – it helps them internalize or understand the action so they are aware of it in the future when they do it.

Drill: Fielding a Ground Ball to Left or Right

Also called the "Goalie Drill"

This is one of my favorite drills as it focuses on good footwork. The idea is to move side to side and shuffle the feet instead of crossing the feet while moving toward the ball. Set up two cones or markers about 20 feet apart and put a player in the middle, while you stand 10-15 feet away. This photo shows the start, with the player already in motion.

Roll the ball to your right; the player has to shuffle to his left and try to get the ball before it goes past the cones and scores a GOAL – one hates to use soccer language in a baseball book, but it works for this drill! Reminds me of my favorite joke: What would hitting be called if it was easy? Answer: Soccer. Sorry, soccer fans ...

Anyway, the players know soccer, so they understand they need to move quickly to keep the ball from rolling past the cones. So roll the ball toward the cone on your right and you will see the player shuffle and get to it:

Now roll the ball to your left. Here you can see the player moving quickly, not crossing the feet, and getting to the ball before it makes it past the cone.

Be sure your players don't cross their feet during this drill. Get them shuffling from side to side, one foot after the other, without crossing their feet.

It's easy for a player to lose balance from this position and it really does not help the player get to the ball. Repeating this goalie drill will help them learn the movements that work and avoid this little pitfall.

To run this drill I normally rotate players as the "goalie" and give them 4 or 5 balls in a row and keep track of how many "goals" they give up. It's usually much fun *and* you will see footwork improve. As players progress you can widen the distance between the cones and increase the speed of the ball.

SKILL C: HITTING

Hitting is, for most players, their favorite thing to do. Who wouldn't want to smash a ball with a big stick?

Teaching hitting is, though, non-trivial to say the least.

Professional baseball players spend much of their offseason watching frame-by-frame records of their swing, changing it, tweaking it, always looking for improvement. For Tee Ball kids, though, all we want is just a few good habits.

First of all, we want the player to hold the bat with two hands, with the hands close together, with the knuckles lined up – this frees up the wrists.

The bat is drawn back with the elbows positioned as if they are resting on a table.

This photo shows the hitting hands being held far apart. It's exaggerated, but some kids will just naturally hold their hands a little too far apart. The key is to make sure players know to put their hands together.

Next, we want the knuckles – the doorknob-knocking knuckles – to be lined up, to free up the wrists. Line them up on the bat.

I have always taught that the knuckles should be aligned and I certainly believe this improves the ability of the wrist to freely move. I do not spent countless hours with really young kids to worry too much about their knuckles, as many with small hands have enough troubles to just get the bat to the ball. As they progress I do correct this, but I think having a good starting bat position with hands together and feet shoulder width apart and knees slightly bent are super important; no need to focus on correcting knuckles.

We want each player to use the lower half of the body to drive the ball. The throwing drills help, as the kids start off facing 90 degrees away from their target – so if the target is due north, the bellybutton is facing east – or west for left-handed players. The same is true for hitting. The batter shouldn't stand there with the bellybutton facing the pitcher, even though at the end of the swing, the bellybutton is indeed facing the pitcher – just like when a player

Focus on the lower half of the body to drive the ball.

throws. The two are related because of the hips; the hips turn, which generates power, which will generate speed. With throwing it's the arm speed and with hitting it's the bat speed.

Step #1: Grip the bat correctly: First of all, we want the player to hold the bat with two hands, with the hands close together, with their knuckles lined up – this frees up the wrists. The bat should be drawn back with the elbows positioned as if they are resting on a table.

At this you can count on hearing parents screaming ELBOW UP – GET YOUR ELBOW UP! But this "elbow up" position is really **not** needed, and don't fight the parents who harp on it. Just don't teach it to the kids. The reason it doesn't matter is that the batter has to drop the elbows once the swing is started, so "elbow up" isn't really all that helpful.

It's just one of those things that people believe– and why fight it? Just quietly tell the parents later that it doesn't matter; most good hitting coaches never talk about elbows being up.

The lower half of the body drives the baseball.

When the batter's hands start to move toward the ball, the hips turn, and that generates the speed and power needed to whack the ball. Most Tee Ball kids at first just swing with their arms, and they miss the chance to really HIT the ball. Have them take a stride, just like throwing, and as that lead foot hits the ground, they should turn their back foot (sometimes called SQUISHING THE BUG) and turn the hips. I like to say TURN YOUR HIPS and then grab their hips and turn them so they can feel it.

Step #2: Bring the bat up into hitting position. Get the bat up and off the

shoulder. Show the player how to hold the bat so it's not pointed straight up and down. Make sure the feet are wide and the knees are bent. Toes are pointed straight – this makes sure the hips do not turn before the swing.

This photo shows a player just learning the correct stance and you can see I have all of the other players watching and giving advice.

This is called peer modeling and can be a very effective teaching tool.

It's also good to have players check their distance to the plate. It's important that the bat is able to cover the whole plate.

Here we have a player extend their arms and make sure the bat can touch the outside corner of the plate.

Here's a photo where the bat is not in a good position to hit the ball – it's just straight up, and the knees are not bent.

It's important to build the habit, particularly with kids this age, of getting themselves into a good pre-swing position.

Here's one where the bat is held a little too low and I'm making the correction to raise it up some.

Another mistake players at this age level commonly make is to "wrap" their bat behind their neck so that they now have to move the bat quite a distance to actually get it over to the ball to hit it.

Here's a photo of me grabbing a wrapped bat and showing the player where to hold it. Instead of the bat pointed to his left it should be pointed behind him.

BATTER READY

This is a good ready position, with the knees bent, eyes locked on the pitcher, with the bat in a good position to hit the ball.

Step #3: Swing and turn the back foot. You want kids to use their hips when they swing, and the hips and hands should move together. Make sure they follow through; this ensures the bat doesn't stop at any point during the swing.

As the swing starts, bring the hands to the ball quickly. The barrel of the bat is on a plane with the ball, and the hips have turned to drive the bat to the ball.

Right after contact, with the player's eyes right on the ball.

Follow-through is HIGH here, and the front side is STRONG.

Note in each photo the hips are turning; they're moving with the hands, which are spaced correctly on the bat. Follow-through by this player is excellent, and the back foot is turning.

Here is a player *who is just missing a ball* and you can see his head has "pulled" off the ball and he's no longer looking at the ball; the back foot has not completely turned.

But why did this happen?

The eye-hand coordination is the key to the whole thing. The eyes see the ball and the brain uses this information to project where the ball will be by the time it gets close to the player; watching the ball's path gives the brain the best information. When the player swings, if the eyes are not on the ball, then the player is just guessing where the ball is.

The best hitters in baseball always say they can see the ball hit the bat and I believe them. When I hit, I do not see the ball hit the bat, but the more I try to follow the ball to the point of contact, the better I am able to hit a moving ball. The eyes can be trained to follow the ball, and the more reps players get seeing the ball and following it, the better batters they will be. Sometimes it's useful just to have players stand in a batting stance without swinging, with their eyes following the ball as it is thrown.

The goal of turning the back foot is to product back-side rotation; the back foot turning means the hips are turning, and if the timing is right then the player is generating bat speed with the whole body, instead of just swinging with the hands.

This player is getting better and has some back-side rotation, but certainly could have more – and his head has pulled off the ball. The key drills to address these points are "cement feet" for head pulling and "bat behind the back" for turning the back foot. Remember that having players freeze at the end of a swing is a great way to make small corrections and show them what needs improvement.

Have them swing many many times without a tee – the tee at this point is merely a distraction. Don't push them past improvement and into boredom, but get it close!

One season I bought ten 13-ounce bats for $50. They were cheap and plastic, but they were labeled Tee Ball bats. I had every player just stand on a line and do the steps and swing. **Step 1:** Hands together, **Step 2:** Arms back, **Step 3:** Stride, **Step 4:** Squish bug, **Step 5:** SWING

Here the batter is set, the knees are shoulder width, and the eyes are on the pitcher. Batter is standing at a good distance from the plate.	*The swing starts, and the hips and hands are moving at the same time.*	*Eyes locked on the ball, and the head has not turned.*

Remember, it's 900 reps to get a good swing. We do not need a tee here – everyone on the team can get in the reps together – just line them up and get them swinging.

This little problem is easy enough to prevent – it's kids using a bat that's too heavy. This photo shows the player struggling to swing a bat, which is a common problem in youth sports; someone gives a player a bat for a present, and the player is motivated to use it right away. The arms drop as the players get tired, and then they are dropping their hands and swinging *up* at the ball instead of swinging on a level plane *to* the ball.

Once they are swinging and it's become almost natural to them with no bad habits, then we can introduce them to the tee. Start by measuring the height of the tee; this photo shows a player making sure the tee is at bellybutton height. Next place the tee a little in front of home plate (not ON home plate) so that the contact point will be out in front of the plate and not immediately over the plate. If a player waits to swing till the ball has crossed half of the plate, the ball will be very hard to hit. Many coaches put the tee right *on* home plate as it seems to match, but for tees with a pole in the middle, this is just not going to work well.

The top of the tee should be at the bellybutton level, but make sure the batter stands back so the bat's contact point is at the *front* of the plate.

This tee has been intentionally placed very poorly. It is right ON home plate.

Ideally at this point, you can get a few tees and have a few players hit off them in the outfield of your practice area away from people – like a driving range away from the other players – and get in as many reps as you can.

One of the parents can position a ball on the tee and announce the 5 steps for the player.

Once they start hitting well, you can just say two of them: STEP and SWING, and when the kids are consistently doing it right you can say just SWING.

It's a good idea to use tennis balls for this so no one gets hurt by a hit ball, and be sure you use just lightweight bats – no more than 15-ounce bats no matter what, and preferably a bit lighter. Bat length should be 24 or 25 inches

at most for most kids. In baseball parlance this is called a DROP 10 – because the length is 25 and the weight is 15 (to all scientists, please forgive us baseball people for mixing units of measure). You can buy DROP 11 or DROP 12 bats (signified by a -10, -11, -12 on the bat) but they get more expensive. A DROP 10 is fine; I very much prefer a 13-ounce 23-inch bat.

Many bad habits are developed by giving kids bats that are too heavy – just don't do it! When the ball is on the tee you should talk to the player about hitting line drives to the pitcher or beyond, and tell them about bat speed and about hitting with power. Keep in mind that many kids are not apt to swing very hard, and they need to be encouraged to do it – it just takes a lot of reps.

Drill: Dry swings practice

Line the players up and have them all practice dry swings. No tee and no ball – just recite the 5 steps and make swings, fine-tuning each step as you watch the kids swing.

Drill: Swing with two balls on two tees

This is a very effective drill. Set out a pair of tees, as close together as possible, and set a ball on each one so they're both on a line from the catcher to the pitcher – or where they would be if you had a catcher and a pitcher. Position the balls close together and have the player hit both balls in one swing. This will get the kids to stay level for a little extra time. If they hit one ball or the other, you get a quick diagnostic of what's going on. If they hit the first ball but not the second one, they are usually chopping at the ball like an axe or using a big upper cut – starting at the bottom and swinging up. Major league players use a *slight* upper cut, but let's save that for the older players! These are Tee Ball kids and we want a nice level swing that generates pleasant line drives.

Drill: Windshield wipers

Hold the bat up and bring it to the left and then to the right – like a car's windshield wipers. This is a great way to build arm strength, and it also gets the player used to holding a bat. You can do this as a warmup – spread your team out in a big circle with one player per bat and have them practice this for several reps at every practice. Encourage them to practice this at home by telling them *how it builds strength and makes them into power batters.*

Drill: Stance with no swing

Working on the stance is important in developing good batting habits, and good batting habits means good hitters. If the feet are too close together or too far apart, or if the knees are locked or the hands are too high or too low, there is really no hope of consistently hitting the ball. If the body is turned the wrong way (too much toward the catcher or too much toward the pitcher), that player has little hope of hitting the ball.

You have to teach muscle memory for the stance.

To start, have the players stand with hands behind their backs so you can focus on the lower half of the body.

Start with the feet at shoulder width apart, knees bent, and weight slightly forward. Its tough to get young players to lean forward without putting too much weight forward; just remind them they should not be straight up and down.

Here's a photo where the player is not leaning forward. Get them to lean into it just a bit, then clap and say STRIDE and the player strides toward the pitcher.

Not a big step, and not a stomp, but a light stride, a step. I usually mirror this for players so if they are right-handed I act like I'm left-handed. I usually CLAP and say STRIDE and then I stride and they stride with me.

Now I clap and say TURN THE BACK FOOT -- I used to say SQUISH THE BUG but some coaching books were concerned that caused too much of a SQUISHING and not even back-side rotation – which really just means the hips need to turn. This pic shows the back foot is turned. The hips have rotated and good things will happen.

Once they get the hang of this with the hands behind the back, you can add the hands and an imaginary bat so they can practice the next stage.

You can line the kids up for this one, or (briefly) work with them one at a time so the others can see what you're talking about. Tell them to not pick up a bat; just CLAP your hands and say READY – and have them get their feet into the proper position. Show them the right position and the wrong positions. You can put a cone in front of them – better yet is a portable cheap plastic home plate or a base – and have them get into the correct batting stance. They should get their feet wide, with their knees slightly bent, weight on the balls of the feet, with their head locked right onto the imaginary tee.

Just because the lower half of the body moves doesn't mean the batter's head has to move.

Then you say SET and they should bring their hands up as if they are holding a bat. Then you say SWING and they should swing the imaginary bat and squish the imaginary bug with the rear foot – and then freeze there at the end of the swing. You want them to freeze *so their body learns how it feels* and you can go around and make corrections and little adjustments with their bodies frozen.

They may not notice something they're doing "almost right" when they come out of the swing, but if you get them to freeze there, they will notice, and you will notice, and together you can fix it!

After this, tell them RESET and do it all again. Ten of these at a time is a really helpful thing to do before you even put bats in their hands.

Drill: Cement Feet

This is a great drill for players whose heads turn every time they swing. Separating upper body from lower body is not easy for players (especially at this age). Just because the lower body is moving doesn't mean the head has to move – at all. Tell the players to keep their heads still and swing – *and don't move their feet at all*. This just builds some muscle memory around not moving their head while swinging a bat. After they've done a few repetitions of this, have them move their feet and then see if their head still turns. If it does, return to cement feet and rinse and repeat.

Drill: Bat Behind Back

This drill is all about teaching the hips to turn. Put the bat at hip level behind the player's back, and have them hold it there with their hands. Then say STEP and the player takes a step toward the pitcher; then say TURN and the back foot turns. The bat can help the back foot turn by having the player pull on the bat. As players progress with this, get them to *not collapse their front foot* as they turn. Ideally, as the front stride foot lands, it pushes against the ground and helps turn the stride-foot-side of the hip. For a right-handed batter, the left foot strides, pushes back, and straightens the knee – and as this stride foot hits the ground, the right foot turns, which will turn the right side of the hip, which is helped by the left hip turning as well. Many young players lack the muscle strength needed to keep the stride foot from collapsing, so be patient with this, let them understand the foot should stay put (eventually), and as time permits work on some strength and conditioning of the quads and hamstrings to help make this move doable.

Drill: Whiffle ball pitch / Tennis ball pitch

This drill is primarily to **reduce fear of the ball**. As players progress out of Tee Ball, fear of the ball is the killer for many players. They aren't sure where the ball is going, so their brain suggests they get out of the way! Even when players are coached not to worry, they still flinch. The key is to start slowly with tennis balls from a close distance, and then gradually work your way backward, thus lengthening the pitch.

The problem with baseballs is that if you throw them from a close distance, the player may actually hit one and hurt a coach. As a coach, you need to be very aware when you are tossing balls to a player holding a metal bat. Just because they don't seem like they will ever hit one, the light can come on at any time, and BANG you are ducking for your life. As players get bigger, you should use an L-Screen to protect yourself, but at very young levels the problem of fear of the ball is really not addressed enough.

An effective thing to do is fake a throw a few times and see if they flinch. If they do, you will see it and they can recognize it, so you both can fix it. Be very patient, and remember that most players grow out of ball fear eventually and it's a lot like riding a bike – as they get over the fear they develop the muscle memory and ball fear eventually becomes a non-issue. At the young levels, though, it's a very big issue and most coaching books do not address this. The reason they don't is that there isn't really all that much you can do about it, other than using softer balls and starting close and working your way back. A bit of work with players on catching fly balls will also help. If players can't *track* a ball that's thrown to them, they will have a hard time hitting it.

For whiffle balls and tennis balls I recommend using a Swiftstick or something like it – partly because a light bat enables numerous swings.

Check out this photo where SIX players are all hitting at the same time. At most practices I see coaches with one player hitting at a time, usually at home plate where the coach throws to them. Young kids can watch only so much of this before they're bored silly, but they'll stand there for a surprisingly long time to practice swinging with you.

One kid at a time is fine as players get older and master the basics,

Most kids just naturally grow out of fear of the ball. Tossing tennis balls from a short distance is one of the few things you can do to help.

but to instill some good habits at a young age, it's so much better to get in 25-50 swings in 20-25 minutes using whiffle balls or tennis balls.

Note that this takes LOTS of assistant coaches. You can see that I'm behind the hitters walking the line, retrieving a few balls and able to make some coaching points on batters, but I can focus on that only because I have SIX assistants at this practice throwing pitches. Now you can really see what I mean by the WHOLE VILLAGE approach! In addition to those six, we also had another coach retrieving balls. So really this scene was eight coaches working a drill with six players.

Drill: Soft Toss Game

In this drill I do a soft toss, which is where you start on one knee and toss the ball to the batter. Show the batter the ball, and then bring your arm back and let the ball roll off your fingers. Try to aim for a spot out in front of the plate, so the batter can stride and hit the ball. Do not just toss the ball over the plate, because the contact point should really be in front of the plate. If you toss it over the plate, it will be very hard for the player to hit. Just watch a kid stepping into it and reaching to hit a ball, and you'll see that this is the more natural and productive movement for them to try.

With players in the field, play the ball as if it is a real pitch. You can have parents as outfielders and play a game with five players on each team and everyone will have fun. You don't get as many reps as a good batting drill, but alas some of these good batting drills can just be too boring. If all you do is boring drills, your team will revolt. Try to mix in some fun along with the boring and try to make the boring fun – by emphasizing how important good hitting is to the game. Teams that don't score any runs have a hard time doing much at all.

SKILL D: RUNNING BASES

Running the bases is not a natural athletic skill that young kids just automatically know how to do. They need to learn a few basics to be able to run around the diamond, and you can help them smoothly through the process with a bit of guidance and practice.

Talk to your players about where to run and the importance of running in a straight line. Have them run the bases before and after each practice. Most Tee Ball coaches do this one pretty well, and there's not much to it, but it does need some practice. Save your little players the embarrassment and make SURE they know the route from home base around the field and back to home base.

DON'T FORGET to make it clear to them – repeatedly – that it's okay to run through first base, and to run though home, but they have to STOP at second and third! This seems incredibly simple to us adults, but you might be surprised at the number of little kids who don't yet grasp this concept.

Drill: Run to first

Have each player stand at home. Tell them GO and have them assume a batting stance, pretend to hit a ball, and then run to first.

Make sure they know they have to run on the right side of the foul line. They should run *through* first and then immediately turn around to the *right* and show absolutely no intention of going on to second base.

As they cross first base, if they get good at it, have them break down their speed by taking a few short steps. As they progress, tell them to watch the first base coach, who will point to the foul line if they're supposed to stop at first, or will point to second bas if they are supposed to keep running.

Drill: Start one on second and another at home

Start a runner on second base with another runner on home plate. Have them race from there to home and second base, so they can practice taking good turns around first and third base.

SKILL E: KNOW WHAT TO DO WHEN YOU GET THE BALL

Drill: Where's the play?

Talk to your players about a force-out, what it is and where it might happen, and then run a drill with runners on base. Put one on first and set up the defense. Say WHERE'S THE PLAY and when they answer TWO then hit a ground ball to the pitcher for the throw to second base. Fielders can also practice the CREEP CREEP SHOW before you make the swing.

When you yell WHERE'S THE PLAY they should answer ONE for a play at first, TWO for a play at second, THREE for a play at third, and FOUR for a play at home.

Do this same simulation drill for other situations, yelling WHERE'S THE PLAY and getting them to call it correctly and play it that way.

- No runners – the play's at ONE
- Runner on first – the play's at TWO
- Runners on first and second – the play's at THREE
- Bases loaded – the play's at FOUR

And that's really all you need for Tee Ball!

Before every batter in every game, yell at the team WHERE'S THE PLAY. Eventually some of them will start yelling this, and eventually they'll start yelling at each other PLAY'S AT TWO!

COVERING BASES

Drill: Ground ball to pitcher, throw to first

Pretty close to 99 percent of plays in Tee Ball and Coach Pitch are a ground ball to pitcher who then throws to first base. Practice this by rolling the ball to the pitcher, who fields it cleanly and throws it accurately to first base.

The pitcher needs to bend the knees to get to the ball and set their feet and then throw to first. Count this down from 4 to 1 as you do it – most fields in youth baseball allow four seconds to make a play. This varies based on lots of factors, but four seconds is a good number to use. You can start at 6 or 7 if you need to, count it down so they get the concept, and then lower your countdown to 4 as they develop physically enough to actually achieve this.

Most plays during a game of Tee Ball — actually in Coach Pitch also — consist of a ground ball hit toward the pitcher, who throws to first base. Practice this with all your players.

CATCHING FLY BALLS

This is a really tough skill for youngsters, because the player has to be aware that the ball is hit, figure out that it's coming at them, and then catch it – and that is a tall order for a Tee Ball player. I recommend you limit practice on this skill until maybe the last three practices of the season. In Coach Pitch, work on this in the middle of the season and in Kids Pitch, start right away; catching becomes a much bigger deal at that level and the players are all able to do it.

Catching a fly ball is just not a thing that will happen much in a Tee Ball game, and many little kids will just DUCK if they see a ball coming at them without

warning! There isn't much positive reinforcement you can provide now for catching a fly ball – most kids at age 5 or 6 just can't do it.

In this photo the player is really tracking the ball and not getting his feet tangled up as he moves toward it.

It's important here to practice quality repetitions. Start close with a tennis ball and no glove, and gradually advance to a baseball and a glove. Toss the ball softly and not too high, and then you will see the player start catching it. If the player's head is not tracking the ball and the eyes are not tracking the ball, don't make a big deal out of this, just try a few minutes of this action every now and then.

Drill: Tennis Balls

Have the player stand 5 feet away from you; get on your knees so you're at their level, and then gently toss them a tennis ball, right into their hand. Fake the throw a few times and you'll see why: many kids will react by stepping back even before you throw it. *They know it might hurt if it hits them,* and they also know they have no idea where that ball is going to land or when – so they are eager to get out of the way.

Try to work them out of this habit of stepping back before the ball is thrown. Have them stand with their back to a wall or a fence so they physically can't step back, and gradually their body will lose the "back away from the ball" habit. You can toss the ball just a little short, too, so they get the idea that they might actually need to lean forward a bit to catch it. When they start catching the ball and you can see they're tracking it, then you can toss the ball a little higher and let them step back to get it.

One helpful thing to work on this is to have another player stand behind the player who is about to catch the ball.

The photo here shows my niece standing behind my nephew with a hand on his back just so he remembers to move forward and not back. Try it.

Just having a hand on the player's back removes some of the instinct to immediately back up when the ball is thrown. Overcoming that very natural reaction is one of the hardest things for the new young player. The gentle reminder they get when they back into someone else's hand is a quick way to teach this without complicating it by having them think about this AND the ball AND the feet.

Be patient and remember there aren't too many 15-year-olds who immediately take a step back when the ball is thrown – they do eventually get it, but you can help that player by having them learn this early. It's all eye-hand coordination and tracking the ball.

When players know they can catch the ball, they will stop moving away from it. Remember, it is a very natural fear to move backward away from a hard object coming at you.

Practice with some fake throws and work at it tirelessly and you'll find that once the catching does start, it doesn't stop.

Note in these photos the fingers pointed to the sky for both hands and the bare hand is ready to cover the ball as soon as it is caught.

As they get better you can teach them that for balls they catch above their waist they should turn their glove to a backhand position (right) and for balls below the waist it's better to use a forehand position (with glove held like photo above).

Drill: Catching on Knees

Set the players up on both knees and then toss them the ball. Taking out the lower half of the body reduces the complexity of the action, and they can focus on catching without worrying whether the feet are stepping back or not. Start with no glove and when they've got that then add a glove.

Start close and gradually move backward.

Also feel free to just stand up and drop a ball and see if they can track it. Sometimes I do this standing on a bench and dropping balls so they have a little more time. This removes the variance of how you throw the ball and they can just focus on only the ball and catching it.

Drill: Helmet Fun

Have one of your players put on a helmet with a full cage mask and then try to get the tossed tennis ball to hit the helmet cage. *Kids love this*, and after a while they will be eager to do it.

Usually we have two kids at a time do this, and we play it for points. The pair of them get 1 point if the ball hits the helmet, 3 points if it hits the cage, and 5 points if they can get the ball to stick in the cage (there is usually a gap between the top of the cage and the helmet). It's pretty tough to get a 5-pointer but it'll happen every now and then, much to everyone's delight.

Drill: Players on the fence with no glove

Arrange your players with their backs to the fence, so even if they are afraid of the ball they won't step back. Toss the ball gently and have them catch it with no glove. This ensures they have their fingers to the sky. Players throw the ball up on their own and then catch it.

First get them ready, off the fence, with fingers pointed to the sky.

Here you can see the player's eyes right on the ball with fingers pointed to the sky.

Drill: Wide Receiver

This is one of my favorites and it will be yours too. Set up a cone about 15 feet from the player's start position, and have them run to the cone and then turn toward either their left or right (up to you), then throw them a fly ball as if they are a wide receiver in football running for a catch (in football it's known as a down-and-out). This forces them to track the ball. It's a great "gathering" drill as you can do this with one player or ten players.

Sometimes I just line them up at first base, say GO and have one player run to second base and cut toward third and I toss them the ball – so it lands at about the shortstop position and they try to catch it and then throw it to a coach I have positioned at third. Then they touch third and run home, then back to the end of the line at first base.

I call it a "gathering" drill because if some players are a couple of minutes late to practice I can still get started and I can even get some reps in a couple of minutes before practice. Nothing worse than a bunch of kids sort of standing around waiting for practice to begin.

Be the first on the field, and just get started with whoever shows up. I can't always be the first but I try to talk to an assistant and tell them the gathering drill should start as soon as the first kid arrives. It sets the tone that practice is not a time to just stand around, and those who show up first get to start first.

This photo is my youngest son when he was 8 heading to the cone and then starting to track the ball.

This is a great drill to teach tracking of the ball, and if you run it every day you'll see big dividends by the end of the season. Just run it for 5-10 minutes at the start of practice.

You can vary the complexity by throwing it higher for players who are getting the hang of things and throw it a little lower for players who aren't yet tracking well. Use very soft balls or tennis balls when players are just getting started – and also do this with no gloves if no one can catch at all, because gloves just get in the way of catching when players first start it.

PITCHING

The number one search query that brings people to my coaching website at CoachingYouthBaseball.com is "teaching pitchers." Why? Because a friendly coach who has just done Tee Ball and coach pitch and is now looking at a season on kid pitch will probably say OH GOOD HEAVENS HOW AM I GOING TO GET LITTLE PLAYERS TO THROW STRIKES?!?

I strongly recommend reading the referenced sources on pitching at the end of this book, and watching the recommended videos. For this book, I just completed a season of kid pitch, and we ended up with about eight players pitching – and of those eight about four really threw strikes consistently, even with all my impressive knowledge and experience with pitching – and having attended numerous pitching clinics, read the books, interviewed college and pro pitchers, and studied frame-by-frame videos made by pitching experts.

Seriously, have of them consistently threw strikes, and lots of pitchers don't really throw all that many strikes. This year we did have a few who threw really well as the season progressed, and that's why we finished with only one loss – as close as it gets to undefeated – but I cannot claim to be anything like the great magician of teaching youth pitching.

What I can do, though, is teach you what I know. I can definitely say that if the kid cannot throw a ball 46 feet to a target, there is no hope of that kid throwing 46 feet to a catcher in a game. There are very few sports that put so much pressure on one player as baseball does to a pitcher.

So first, do all the drills in the throwing section frequently until you have some players who can consistently throw 46 feet from where they stand to the target.

When I start working with a pitcher, we stand 10-15 feet apart and I just say step and throw. They immediately do a great big windup like Juan Marichal (if you don't know him, just go search on YouTube, as he was the poster child for the big leg-kick). They want to show you how they know all about pitching.

Start, weight on balls of feet, knees slightly bent, glove within a couple of inches of the chest and eyes locked on the target.

Balance point. Small leg lift. Player must be balanced here and not wobbly.

Stride and turn back foot, which turns hip.

Elbow is above shoulder with good stride length.

Notice back is bent, which means the back is really involved in throwing the ball.

Pitching motion ends with the rear leg coming even with the front leg and the pitcher turns into a fielder. This is super important at the early levels in kid pitch as many, many balls will come right back to the mound.

The sequence of photos here illustrates some key checkpoints when working with young pitchers. First the pitcher starts out in what is called the "stretch" position facing third base. I recommend this for all new pitchers. Next is a small, balanced leg lift to bring players into the balance point. Make sure pitchers do not wobble at this point, and if they do, lower the leg lift until they don't. Next you can see the pitcher's hip turn, and a good long stride. Some books recommend a stride of as much as 80 percent of body length. Many young pitchers use almost no stride at all, and it really hurts them. Finally, the pitcher's back is bent as part of the throw and he ends up as a fielder.

I tell kids when they're starting out to skip the leg kick and just step and throw. Getting rid of a big leg lift is the first step to success – if a player is at 70 percent strikes then you can experiment a little with a leg kick, but for young players it's just too much. It usually causes them to lose their balance, and without balance heaven help you to throw a strike. I would say getting rid of the leg kick was actually the key to two of our best pitchers.

Also, teach your pitchers that after every pitch they walk toward home 3-5 steps and reduce the distance from the catcher. Even MLB pitchers do this, clear up to the World Series level, so it's just fine if your little pitchers do it.

If you don't teach them this, it's likely you will end up in a miserable situation in a game where the pitcher throws the ball to the catcher who misses it, and then the catcher throws it back to the pitcher who misses it, and people have to watch grass grow throughout this whole performance.

After every pitch, remind the catcher to come up some, and remind the pitcher to come toward the catcher, until it's a habit for both of them. The last thing you need for little pitchers is for them to get worn out running around chasing balls returned from the catcher. Many young catchers just chuck the ball over the pitcher's head – and it's an important teaching moment that *one of the catcher's most important jobs is to make life easier on the pitcher.*

Drill: Stride toward home, come back and throw

With this drill you have the pitchers start in the *stretch* position with their glove-side shoulder directly lined up with home. (The *wind-up*, conversely, is when the pitcher's bellybutton faces home. This is absolutely not needed at the first levels of kid pitch; it merely adds complexity where none is needed.) Have your kids pitch from the stretch at all times.

I have players start with their feet shoulder-width apart and then stride toward home (no leg kick, just a stride) and then come back to the set position and then stride toward home and throw. The stride, return and stride again is in a lot of books and it seems to help pitchers make sure they are stepping on a line. If you can bring some rope or are able to draw a line on the field where players can stride it's a good thing, as most young pitchers either step a little to the right of home or to the left, and the best results occur when they get their stride foot to land directly on the path to home.

Here's a photo of a pitcher – my oldest son at age 10 – who didn't pitch much because velocity didn't really happen for him until he got older. I rarely talk about ball velocity because I think it has a lot to do with fundamental strength and conditioning and not so much with mechanics.

But you can see his front foot is directly on the line to the plate. He has his elbow above the shoulder and he has his glove in front of his body (see throwing section). His head is facing the plate and his eyes are on the target.

Drill: Step behind and throw

Come into the set position, take a long step toward home with the front foot, bring the back leg behind the front leg and stride and throw. This generates some momentum before the pitch and gets players to feel what it's like to generate some arm speed.

Drill: Game Simulation

Once you think a pitcher can throw strikes, have them throw against live batters at practice. Give them 20 pitches and tell them at least 10 need to be strikes. Allow batters to hit the ball. You can do this even if you have a game the next day – 20 pitches is recognized as being a good number.

Drill: High-5 drill

Have the player step toward the plate and throw – with no ball. Stand in front of them and put your hand out and have them slap your hand as you hold it out for them. Many players will not bend their backs when they throw or follow through. Holding your hand out for a high-5 like slap ensures that they have to keep moving the throwing arm even after the pitch.

Drill: Towel Drill

Have the pitcher hold a towel between the thumb and forefinger, then step and throw. Instead of using a ball, get them to throw and snap the towel. If they are pushing the ball the towel won't do anything, but a good throw will require them to PULL the towel and good things will happen.

THE FINE ART OF RUNNING A FANTASTIC PRACTICE

Anyone can run a crummy practice – even a half-decent practice – but running a high-energy practice takes both time and preparation. Remember, the goal is not to just run around and generate repetitions – it's to generate QUALITY REPS. If these plans are too hectic for your team and your assistants, just slow them down. Cut a station if you need to, and stay focused on technique and repetitions – quality reps.

In this next section you'll find three practice plans – one is for the first couple of practices, one is for the mid-season practices, and one is for the last couple of practices in your season. Vary these plans based on the players you have and their skills – and how many of them show up for practice. If you really care about practice planning you'll see how important it is to know which players and which coaches will be helping out at practice.

You can assume you'll have 10 players at five 2-player stations. If you have a 1-hour practice one day a week, make it a high-energy practice. Get there early. You should schedule a "gathering drill" beginning 10 minutes before practice time, wrapping it up when you actually have enough players to start. The last thing you want is players randomly running around with balls and bats as you wait for the rest of the players to trickle in. Also consider that when players arrive "on time" or late, they (and their parents) will see the kids who arrived earlier *already engaged in practice* on the field, thus encouraging all of them to arrive earlier next time. This one little thing is a key factor in getting them to show up on time and wanting to start, with enthusiasm for both the team and the practice.

The moment a player shows up, they should see that you already have a gathering drill running. Tell them as they arrive, LET'S GO. This sets the tone for practice – this isn't time to just sit around and look at grass or lazily toss a ball around with your dad. We are heading into a *classroom* here and we will be LEARNING THINGS with HIGH ENERGY.

The following practice plans indicate during which minutes (from -10 to 60) each practice segment should happen. Before printing these, you should change the times to match the actual time of day of your practice.

You can download free Quick-Start Guides here:

CoachingYouthBaseball.com/quick-start-guides-landing/

The moment your kids show up at practice, they should see that you already have a gathering drill underway. Tell them as they arrive, "Let's go!"

Practices at the Tee Ball stage often resemble a 4-ring circus with many stations going, so everything must be orchestrated as close to perfectly as you can. Without good planning you will waste time, lose out on reps, or end up with some kid getting hit with a ball. If you are nervous about so many stations, you can reduce these plans to three and cut two stations and see how things go. Work up to it if you have to, but try to get to five stations if possible – it's a challenge for you but it makes a huge difference in the quality of the season for the team, and it's just a lot of fun for the kids!

TEE BALL PRACTICE PLANS

Most Tee Ball practices last just an hour, so here are three 1-hour plans, one for early season, one for the mid-season, and one for late season. Note the scheduling of -10 (10 minutes before practice starts) to +5 (5 minutes after start) or +15 (15 minutes after start).

Practice Plan #1: Early Season

-10 to +5 Gathering Drill:

Line up the kids at home plate and have them run one at a time to first base. This is a great way to get them warmed up, and the kids like it. Players who show up late for practice will see that if they had come earlier they would have had more FUN.

+5 to +10 Warmup:

A team warmup sets the stage for the class you are about to teach. *It should be done the same way at every practice, all season long.* Teams that do this develop a noticeable cohesiveness after a while; it also settles kids down a bit before a game.

Line your players up a couple of feet apart and do 5 minutes of calisthenics exercises. Typical exercises for the large muscle groups are jumping jacks, then feet wide and touch your hands to the ground, right foot over left and stretch, left foot over right and stretch, arm circles, big arm circles, and little arm circles.

+10 to +20 Team Throwing:

Team throwing must be done at every practice and every game. It should be practiced with one player to one coach if at all possible, but if the kids have to take turns then do it every day anyway. They should have a few balls at their feet, and they should just be picking them up and throwing them to the target (see throwing drills earlier in the book). You should recite the cues for throwing as noted in the drill and have the players throw. The person catching the ball puts it down and tells the player to pick up a new one. Ideally when you get this all rolling, you as the coach will call out the cues and go around making corrections, but you are not actually engaged in catching balls. You can also have an older sibling or spare teenager run around and get the balls that have missed their targets so everyone isn't lazily walking around to casually pick up balls. Notice that the whole village is working here – you should have all the parents out there catching balls.

+20 to +25 Team Batting:

If you have bats for everyone, hand them out with helmets and get the players standing far away from each other in one line. Have them do dry swings and make sure they always freeze at the end of each swing. Work on stance first and then dry swing after. Again the WHOLE VILLAGE is at work – every player if at all possible is hitting a ball toward a parent.

+25 to +30 Station Set-up:

Explain to everyone how the stations work, and have the kids run to each station. Tell them it's going to be 5 minutes at a station. Have another parent act as timer so you can yell SWITCH, and make sure players know who is going where and which coach is where. They have to understand that they have only 5 minutes, so they need to work fast.

Allow 2 minutes for the players to move between stations, and make sure they *sprint* from one station to the next.

+30 to +35 Station 1:

Fielding ground balls – rolling the ball straight to them, then players scoop it up.

(2-minute station sprint)

+37 to +42 Station 2:

Game simulation. Set up a pitcher's mound cone and a first base in the outfield with one base runner – for this you have three players. Roll the ball to the pitcher and have them throw to first; the runner with the helmet runs to first. Have a coach ready there at first to retrieve missed balls. Remind the fielder to do all the throwing reps that were just covered, and remind the runner to properly run to first as it was covered in the gathering drill.

(2-minute station sprint)

+44 to +49 Station 3:

Ground balls moving to the left and to the right.

(2-minute station sprint)

+51 to +56 Station 4:

Hitting off a tee – one hitter and two fielders, with both fielders working on fielding live balls. Fielders have to be at least 20 or 30 feet away from the tee. Walk the hitter through the hitting steps.

+56 to +60 minutes – use this for a quick game of rundown. Players run between first and second base and coaches throw tennis balls back and forth while the players run to the base away from the ball. All players can do this, and when a player is tagged out they leave the drill and go get a water break. They can come back in after they catch an easy fly ball from a coach on the side. Use TENNIS BALLS for this rundown drill so the players don't all need helmets and no one gets beaned by a parent.

When I was a kid, we called this game "pickle" because the runner is in a pickle. I play this all the time at the end of practice, and after a while kids start asking, "Are we going to have time to play pickle?"

Practice Plan #2: Mid Season

The only real change here is that we cut a ground ball station and turned it into another hitting station, this one with two tees – for twice the hitting

-10 to +5 Gathering Drill

+5 to +10 Warmup

+10 to +20 Team Throwing

+20 to +25 Team Batting

+25 to +28 Station Set-up

+30 to +35 Station 1: Ground balls – rolling the ball straight to them and side to side

+37 to +42 Station 2: Game simulation

+44 to +49 Station 3: A two-tee station. Put balls on two tees and have one player hit to two fielders. Rotate the players after three swings.

+51 to +56 Station 4: Hitting off a tee – one hitter and two fielders with the fielders working on fielding live balls. Fielders should be at least 20-30 feet away from the tee. Walk the hitter through the hitting steps.

+56 to +60 – quick game of rundown.

Practice Plan #3: Late Season

It's now late season, your last couple of practices. Some good habits are starting to form, and no one should be confused when they come to practice. If you had to cut some stations earlier due to lack of time or lack of coaching assistants, hopefully by now you have them. The change here for this late season practice is that we are finally ready to consider trying some fly balls. Also we can cut the team batting from the lineup as they probably have the gist of the batting stance by now – or at least they should. If you still need to work on this, you can certainly make adjustments to this plan.

-10 to +5 Gathering Drill

+5 to +10 Warmup

+10 to +20 Team Throwing

+22 to +25 Station Set-up

+25 to +30 Station #1: Ground balls – rolling the ball straight to them, and side to side

+32 to +37 Station #2: Game simulation

+39 to +44 Station #3: Two-tee station, with two balls on two tees and one player hitting to two fielders. Rotate the players after three swings.

+44 to +49 Station 4: Hitting off a tee – one hitter and two fielders so fielders can work on fielding live balls. Fielders have to be at least 20 feet away from the tee – walk the hitter through the hitting steps.

+49 to +54 Fly balls – do the helmet drill for fun

+56 to +60 Quick game of rundown for fun

Tee Ball Game Management

We don't keep score in Tee Ball, but the games are hot, the kids sometimes miss the tee and a game can be a tough 90 minutes in your life. Let's plan to really get something valuable out of that time: Have your kids show up 30 minutes early for each game, so you can basically run a quick practice. Here's how you do it.

Get there early and figure out your dugout. Set up your station in half of the outfield – no one can be upset about that. Disregard the other team – they are probably just standing around with some kids lazily playing catch with their parents. It's not your problem that other coaches will think you are crazy if you follow this book – they'll keep thinking you're crazy until your team becomes very dominant in a year or two and then they will wonder why you were so LUCKY and you GOT ALL THE BEST KIDS.

They probably still won't admit that this is the very best way to run youth baseball coaching, because it just flies in the face of 50 years of conventional wisdom, i.e. not really running fast-paced, multi-station practices with real preparation. Just stay true to the course, focus on your team and what you're teaching, and don't worry about every other coach's opinion. Just blame it on this book. "Well hey, I got this crazy book and I'm just giving it a TRY."

Here's your game plan for Tee Ball games.

40 minutes before game time – which is 10 minutes before you told them to show up – start the gathering drill of running from home to first.

At -25 minutes before game time, get rolling! Get everyone in the outfield and start team warmups – just like you do in practice. You may be surprised at how quickly your kids settle into this routine. Kids like knowing what comes next, and a game is less scary when you're just doing something familiar. You set the stage for the game – it's nothing special, it's just another way we can get in a few more quality reps and put some things in motion here.

At -20 minutes before game time, finish warmups and set up the TEAM THROWING.

At -5 minutes, declare victory on team throwing, and have your kids get some water and head to the bench. Remind them there is NO ON-DECK CIRCLE, and no one touches a bat at all until a coach hands it to you – and that's gonna be YOU right before you hit the ball!

At the start of the game, on the bench, players sit in batting order. NO ONE CLIMBS THE FENCE, and EVERYONE CHEERS FOR THE TEAM.

RIDDLE THE BENCH WITH PARENTS AND COACHES. Make sure everyone is cheering and keeping the kids from catching bugs or climbing fences. Make certain that the batter is always ready to go bat.

Out on the field you should rotate everyone every three batters. This rotation is good: Catcher should just wear a helmet, so you don't have to deal with putting on a chest protector – at this age it's really not necessary and it just slows things down.

FIELD ROTATION:
Pitcher goes to Catcher
Catcher to RF
RF to CF
CF to LF
LF to 3B
3B to SS
SS to 2B
2B to 1B
1B to P

SHOW THEM IN PRACTICE how this works so they don't get all baffled during a game. If you have other outfielders, just rotate them along in the same pattern. Say you have five instead of three outfielders:

Pitcher goes to Catcher
Catcher to RF
RF to RC
RC to CF
CF to LC
LC to LF
LF to 3B
3B to SS
SS to 2B
2B to 1B
1B to P

Keep track of where they left off in each inning, as you might not remember to switch every three batters, so you can just set them up where they left off the previous inning. For batting, bat them in order of uniform number, so it's easy to line them up on the bench. There's no strategy here, no cleanup hitter, all that is for another day. They will get there soon enough.

In the field, talk to them about the ready position and CREEP CREEP SHOW – and have them say the words at each pitch. Yell WHERE'S THE PLAY and get everyone yelling back which base has the play.

If you do get someone out, make it a celebration! Tell your team that you are COUNTING OUTS. That's all – not runs but **outs**. Some teams you play won't want to tell a kid they are out, but try to get the other coach to agree to it, and then be nice to the kid who is OUT – give him high fives or something and be sure your players are with you. Some kids will cry, but alas, this is one of the life lessons we learn about in baseball. Soccer, lacrosse, football, baseball – no one is so *isolated* as in baseball. The kid is out and must now face up to that. Kids are usually okay with this, or they at least get the hang of it – they play games at school or even pre-school where they get OUT and it's okay – they're not a bad person, *the ball just got there first*. So what?

Pay close attention to post-game comments. Have a good snack, have the kids run the whole field at the end, talk to them a lot about what went right, just a little about what went wrong. Tell them all the good things you saw, just a couple things that can be improved. Make sure no one's sidelined and they're all having fun.

DO NOT GIVE OUT A GAME BALL. This is ridiculous. You'll always have two good players who will always deserve the prize and then where is everybody else? So then to make them feel better you end up giving game balls to kids who didn't really do anything – what does that teach? Just skip it – this mistake is commonly made and it teaches *nothing* useful.

COACH PITCH PRACTICE PLANS

With Coach Pitch, there is quite a bit of overlap with Tee Ball, but we do have more time and we can introduce catching more. We can also start players on understanding where the play goes when the ball is hit. We still need plenty of work on the batting tee.

These plans are a hybrid of Tee Ball and Kids Pitch; line-by-line plans would be redundant. If you are coaching Kids Pitch, use the late season Tee Ball plans to start the season, the early season plans from Kids Pitch for mid-season, and the mid-season Kids Pitch plans for late season.

GAME MANAGEMENT:
The night before the game, make a plan that indicates where players will play in each position. Make sure that no player is on the bench more than any other player. Make sure no player is in the outfield more than any other player. Rotate your "pitcher" and your "first baseman" so everyone plays a turn. Most leagues don't keep score at this level, and if that is a rule, make sure it is enforced – keeping score just makes you do things that have nothing to do with player development; for example, putting your best player at first base the whole game.

I strongly encourage you to just keep the batting lineup rolling through the season – if your 8th batter makes the last out in game one, start game two with your 9th batter. I recommend you create your batting lineup by uniform number, so it's easy to figure out who is batting next. Sure, you can spend hours optimizing your lineup and pretend you are a big league manager, but all that will do is reduce at-bats for about a third of the team. *You are here to develop players* so make sure everyone gets the same number of at-bats all season. All your big plans about "putting Johnny at cleanup" so he can bash a bases-clearing home run probably won't happen anyway, so you really aren't losing that much of an edge.

Show up early before games, run the same stretches that you do at every practice, and stick to your before-game routine before every game. For coach pitch, I start with a line of players on the mound, roll the first player a ball and have them set their feet and throw to first or third, whichever base you yell out. Put an assistant coach on first and another on third so you aren't chasing too many balls.

KIDS PITCH PRACTICE PLAN

Early Season

5:15 – 7:00 Goals – improve throwing and pitching – get the kids familiar with footwork involved in pitcher-to-first, and work on some hitting with swift sticks and tennis balls.

5:05 Gathering Drill – wide receiver

5:15 – 5:25 Stretches / relay race

5:25 – 5:30 Water break

5:30 – 5:50 2-line throwing – players throw to coaches – pitching mechanics. Work on a deep breath before the pitch so they focus on the catcher's mitt and then come up and then throw.

5:50 – 5:55 Water break, divide into stations with four players at each station.

Stations: (3 stations with 3 rotations). Rotate LF → Home → RF → LF. The whole station rotates together.

1. 5:55 – 6:10
2. 6:15 – 6:30
3. 6:35 – 6:45

1. **Station 1**: Using the infield: Soft toss game – coach soft-tosses to players and infield tries to make a play on the live ball. P, C, 3B, SS, 2B, 1B – batter – 6 players and 1 coach

2. **Station 2**: GROUND BALLS – use right field: ground ball to the pitcher who throws to first base, with three players and one coach

3. **Station 3**: (4 coaches) Coach throws tennis balls and / or whiffle balls to players with swiftsticks, hitters hitting from the left-field foul line to center field.

6:45 – 6:50 Water break

6:50 – 7:00 Pickle – all players between first and second and two coaches throw tennis balls back and forth. Players run away from the ball and when they are out, they come out till after they catch some balls from an assistant and then they can rejoin.

Mid Season

Here are three plans that we just used in 2021. I'll give you week 1, week 4, and week 8 from a 12-week season. At this point we were ready to increase the emphasis on pitching, and we added a drill teaching catchers to throw to third, as our league allowed players to advance to third on a wild pitch. We inserted a few minutes of kick-ball just for fun. The parents played kickball – I really enjoyed kicking a ball like when I was little – and I'd forgotten how much fun it is! Kudos to our head coach who was in his first year and didn't know that no one ever plays kickball.

5:15 – 7:00 – Goals: improve throwing / pitching – get familiar with the footwork involved in pitcher-to-first and work on some hitting with swift sticks and tennis balls.

5:05 Gathering Drill – Wide Receiver

5:15 – 5:25 Stretches / relay race

5:25 – 5:30 Water break

5:30 – 5:50 2-line throwing – players throw to the coaches – pitching mechanics – work on a deep breath before the pitch, so they focus on the catcher's mitt and then come up and throw.

5:50 – 5:55 water break, divide into stations with four players at each station.

Stations: (3 stations with 3 rotations). Rotate LF → Home → RF → LF. Whole station rotates together.

    1. 5:55 – 6:10
    2. 6:15 – 6:30
    3. 6:35 – 6:45

1: Station 1: Using the infield: Pitcher throws to catcher – catcher throws to 3rd. Two players at pitcher, one catcher, one player at third, one or two coaches

2. Station 2: GROUND BALLS – use RF: GB to P who throws to 1B with four players, one coach

3. (4 coaches) Coach throws tennis balls and /or whiffle balls to players with swiftsticks, hitters hitting from LF foul line to CF

6:45 – 6:50 Water break

6:50 – 7:00 Kickball – kids "bat" continuously until we run out of time, all coaches in the field.

Practice Plan – Late Season

This plan is all about getting players used to hitting off a player pitching. At this point they likely are hitting okay off a coach, but probably are still not confident against kids pitching. Kids know that other kids have trouble throwing strikes. Twenty pitches is a good number to practice without wearing out a player's arm if you have a game the next day, while still getting them some good reps. Count how many strikes they throw and give them good feedback.

4:30 – 6:45 Goals: improve hitting with live pitching

4:30 Gathering Drill – GB SS throw to 2B

4:40 – Stretches

Phase I: Kid pitch

Use the grid below – the players go to the following positions and players on the bench are the hitters for the scrimmage. The pitcher in the next inning starts throwing with a coach in the outfield.

Players pitch 20 pitches each – after that it's just soft-toss for each batter until you reach three outs or two runs. The on-deck batter does soft-toss with a coach. W indicates to warm up the pitcher off to the side of the field and H indicates the batting lineup. For this you need a bench coach to make sure the next hitter is ready. Follow this at 6:35 with some kickball.

#	Player Name	1	2	3	4	5
4	Micky Mantle	7	2	H1	4	9
3	Hank Aaron	W	1	3	5	H1
13	Willie Mays	3	3	8	W	1
1	Lou Brock	6	7	H2	8	6
10	Juan Soto	8	H3	5	H2	4
9	Albert Pujols	5	8	6	H3	7
12	Joe DiMaggio	4	H4	W	1	H2
8	Ozzie Smith	H3	6	7	H4	5
2	Trea Turner	1	H1	H3	2	8
7	Bryce Harper	2	H2	H4	9	2
6	Dave Parker	H4	4	4	7	H3
14	Johnny Bench	H1	W	1	3	3
5	Roberto Clemente	H2	5	2	6	H4

KIDS PITCH GAMES

Finally, you have made it to Kids Pitch, you get to pick who pitches, and that drives the whole game. Now it has become a balance between winning and development. If you pitch only your monster pitchers, the other team doesn't score, your team wins a ton of games, and you sleep easy. The catch is you missed a chance to develop some pitchers. On the flip side, if you just pitch everyone, some players still cannot get the ball to the plate, and the game slows to a very painful crawl, and no one learns anything.

I suggest a happy middle ground. Once players show they can throw 5 out of 10 strikes in a practice, tell them they will pitch. Make sure they can throw strikes to a live batter in practice before putting them in a game – because nothing is going to get easier in a game. In the fall of 2021 our team went 12-1 and pitched all but two players out of a roster of 13. They didn't all pitch at the start, of course, but as the season progressed, more pitchers got a turn. Most of your players can learn to pitch, but you should make pitching in a game a big reward for practice and showing success in practice.

I suggest offering extra practices just to work on throwing and pitching, and that can make a huge difference in getting players really ready to pitch.

As with coach pitch, I suggest a rotating lineup so that all players get the same number of at-bats all season – or as close as you can get to that goal. If you are sure this will hurt your team's success, keep in mind that our team just went 12-1 *and we rotated the lineup all season.* If the 8th batter made the last out, the 9th batted leadoff the next game. This might cost you a little in strategy and you might score more runs by making sure some big hitters are all clustered together at the top, but you do a huge benefit in overall team happiness by involving them all. You don't have players sulking because they are always batting or rarely batting, and that helps team chemistry.

Before the game, I recommend the same stretching routine as done in practice. After stretching, players should throw to each other in two lines for a few minutes. Note that stretching should really come first. Once they have finished throwing, then I suggest making one line at shortstop and one line at second base and hitting groundballs to shortstop and having the second baseman cover second. After the play they go to the end of their lines and the next players in line move up to shortstop and second base. They can have a short throw and they can work on fielding. After a while you can add a first baseman and they can then complete the double play and throw to first.

STORIES FROM YOUTH BASEBALL

These are all real stories, and I could write an entire book on this, but here's a few just for entertainment and to give you an idea of what you can expect. Don't say I didn't warn you.

Story: Why do we get outs?

ME standing next to kid in practice, "How you doing?"

KID: "Okay."

ME: "Cool, you got any questions on anything?" (It was a slow day and I was an assistant coach that day, so practice was running a little slow.)

KID: "Yeah. If I catch the ball what happens to the batter?"

ME: "He's OUT."

KID: "He can't play in the game anymore?"

ME: "Nah, he is just OUT so he can't run the bases for that inning. You get three outs an inning and then you switch. In Tee Ball no one usually gets OUT, so it doesn't come up too much, and even if you get three outs, a lot of leagues let you finish out the batting order."

KID: "Hmm. Well, why do we want to get OUTS?"

ME: "Well if they aren't OUT they can run around the bases eventually and score, which is bad for our team."

KID: "If they score that means they get a point?"

ME: "Well, yes, but please call it a RUN so I can keep my sanity here."

KID: "OH yeah, RUNS, hey, this sounds just like my baseball video game that I play."

ME: "Yep. Well, baseball rules usually don't get changed when they make a video game."

KID: "Oh good, now I get it, since it matches my video game."

ME: "Cool."

Story: Running the wrong way

I set up the fun pickle game with kids running from first to second and another group running from third to home. For some reason one kid got to third and took off running toward second. I can still see it clearly – there was a massive collision. I yelled (probably too loudly) STOP, as I feared the grand collision with all the kids running from first to second. The kid collapsed in a heap right at the shortstop position, sobbing uncontrollably. His parents had to come out and carry him off the field – with them all the while glaring at me. I felt about as bad as anyone can feel.

I can remember it like it was yesterday. I was sure that kid wouldn't play again, and he pretty much avoided me for most of the rest of the season, and his parents just pretended they didn't see me. I was so happy when I saw that kid at a majors game a few years later! The dad chatted with me some, and I apologized again ... and he said it was FINE ... but I could tell he was still irked at the whole memory. When you coach enough, you'll do a lot of things right, but you won't remember many of those. You are cursed to remember the bad ones. Most seasoned coaches can tell you about mistakes they have made – and you just have to accept this and understand that you're gonna do it.

Story: Tee Ball kid smashed with a bat

This one was so sad – at a game one Saturday a 10-year-old was swinging his bat in the non-existent on-deck circle. A little Tee Ball kid walked up behind him and the older kid never saw him. The Tee Ball kid was hit in the face. I was the commissioner at that time and I was summoned to come over and see what was up.

The kid had blood pouring out his mouth and nose, and I asked if someone could quickly find Dr. Johnson – one of our parents who was a doctor. Someone did. A bunch of moms started bringing me paper towels to stop the bleeding, along with a couple boxes of Band-Aids. The kid was screaming, and as I got the blood cleared away before the doctor ran up, I could see that the bat had smashed into his lip and his lip now had a small hole in it where his tooth had bit through his lip. I got the kid to lie down – I told people to find his parents and let them know he was heading to the emergency room ASAP – this was not a little cut.

Everyone was quite shocked that someone could actually get this badly hurt from a young kid practicing with a bat! The older kid was just mortified, so after we got the younger one off with his parents to the emergency room, I walked over and told the older kid that he should have been coached better and that I had told all the coaches a thousand times that there was no on-deck circle, but they tend to think it's just someone being overly cautious or something. Being right about being concerned about bats, though, does NOT make you feel any better. Talking to the parents, it was easy to see they thought the commissioner was somehow at fault here. I'm not sure what else I could have done, but it was a moment I'll never forget. At every Tee Ball game I go to, I see kids taking practice swings, and it brings fear to my heart every time. **There's no on-deck circle, and there's no practice swings.** No exceptions. Most youth baseball organizations have these as clear policies. It's just far too dangerous. Do not allow it.

Story: Kid climbing a fence

Game #1 of the season. There's only one mom on the bench, and you need about four parents there.

One kid on the bench happily climbs the fence, while the mom is supposed to be covering the bench. She looks at the boy and says, "Now Johnny, we don't want to start a precedent here by climbing the fence."

I laugh to myself thinking, REALLY, like this 5-year-old kid knows the word PRECEDENT. Well, the mom didn't get his attention – she used her nice quiet indoor voice. News Flash, boys and girls, we are OUTDOORS now. The kid wasn't paying any attention to her at all and indeed had no idea he was even being talked to – let alone understanding her remark about the word PRECEDENT.

I walked over and barked HEY, GET OFF THE FENCE – and the kid hopped off – and I said NOW SIT ON THE BENCH – and he did – and the mom looked at me in horror. I had not used my indoor voice, and maybe the child is now scarred for life.

It is okay for coaches to speak clearly, and it is okay for them to get a player's attention. It is okay because it's expected to have players respond appropriately to a coach – even if that coach is somebody else's mom! All of this instills discipline, which is a key part of teaching – one can't teach in a classroom where everyone is jumping around climbing random furniture or fences.

Do not be afraid to be in charge – YOU ARE THE COACH. See previous page about kids who take a bat to the face. I'm also a bit touchy about fences, because I had a great kid climb a backstop one afternoon after practice. He fell and broke his wrist and was out for the whole season. I let him climb it, see, because the parents thought it was fun and it was after practice. But after that fun turned to a season-long injury, I was not okay about anyone ever climbing a backstop or a fence.

I guess if you coach for 20 years then you get so many odds and ends in injuries that you end up being kind of a tyrant about safety, but that's okay. Part of a coach's job is to keep all the kids uninjured and everyone safe – and climbing fences is really not such a safe activity. You can have kids and parents make fun of you for being unnecessarily strict about safety rules, or you can have kids and parents make fun of you for not being strict about it when a kid is seriously hurt. Take your pick.

Story: Fundraising

Many leagues do some kind of fundraising. I have found that the best teams I have had, who are winners on the field, often win at fundraising too. It's all part of being on a team. If you just mail in your check and don't raise any money as a team effort, you are sort of telling your team it's okay not to care about or put any effort into team things.

My favorite was one kid who said, "Well, I didn't sell candy bars door-to-door because we just moved in here and we just DON'T KNOW THAT MANY PEOPLE." But that's the whole point – fundraising is all about knocking on doors; you can't just sell stuff to people you know (or get your parents to sell stuff to their co-workers). I asked the kid if it was trick-or-treating would he have just skipped it because he didn't know that many people yet. Oh no, he said, that's different!

Story: Being corrected

Coaches spend their lives being corrected. Some parents who may have played ball in college or even in the big leagues know a LOT more than the average coach, and they really try to avoid a confrontation, but sometimes they can't help it.

I had a Tee Ball team one year and I was doing the throwing drill. A mom came up to me one day and said, "I can't take it anymore. That is not how you throw. I played softball in college, and you do not extend your arm back, you just keep your hand by your ear."

"Well, the reality is," I told her, "that is how we teach catchers to throw so they can get a quick release. But in baseball, especially on a big field, you have plenty of time to throw, so the distances are farther and we need full extension. And when we teach them to pitch we're gonna want full extension. Softball pitchers throw underhand, so it's just different."

She nodded and seemed to accept this, but then a week later she came back and said, "I have looked into this and you are right." I remember this well, as I was so surprised to be corrected on throwing – it is one of my favorite things and I have talked to all sorts of pitchers, pitching coaches, high school coaches, major league pitchers, you name it, to try to learn the details and finer points of throwing and teaching throwing. I have watched a zillion videos of frame-by-frame, and I have filmed my pitchers and broken them down frame by frame. I think I have the basics down. For this mom to question me and try to correct me made me want to walk her through *all my grand experience* ... but luckily for me I decided to try to explain myself and see how it went.

I think some coaches get quickly offended when they are corrected. In baseball there are lots of ways to do things – closed stances, open stances, rotational hitting, linear hitting, and variations on everything. Some parents hate it that I'm teaching a cookie-cutter approach. The answer is that if a kid has tremendous success with something other than what I'm teaching and I'm pretty sure they won't get hurt, then I let them do what they are doing. However, most kids benefit from a cookie-cutter approach, and when they get a little older and have the basics down pat, then they can change it up. I have seen enough kids who at first couldn't throw at all, but then just firing that ball across the diamond after a season or two of these throwing drills. I strongly encourage you to read other books, watch more videos, watch other coaches, and keep learning – the more you know about the mechanics of the game, the better you can teach it. Many coaches don't really teach mechanics, other than screaming ELBOW UP when a kid is batting, and that is ironically the one tip that really won't drive success for young players.

Story: Outs

One spring we had the scheduled league pre-season meeting with all the Tee Ball coaches ... and the commissioner told us repeatedly that this year we will enforce OUTS because he wanted the kids to "learn about life lessons" and OUTS are part of the game.

So when the teams took the field, we practiced and practiced and finally in Tee Ball game #3 we made a legitimate out. It was beautiful, a ground ball to short, and our little shortstop flipped gently to the third-base kid who was standing on the bag with runners on both first and second. I leapt up to celebrate like it was the last out of the World Series!

The third-base coach for the other team smiles and looks at me and says, "But we aren't gonna take him off the bases are we?"

I couldn't believe it. I was so sad. I looked at him and said, "Look, we worked really hard on this, and the commissioner said we were doing it, and now all of a sudden you don't want to bother? What do I tell my team when they've worked hard and succeeded – and suddenly it doesn't matter?"

And he said, "IF we take him off the bases he's going to CRY."

"Tell you what," I replied, "how about we let him stay on the base this one time, and you talk to your team between innings and tell them how we play with outs after this."

He agreed, and I immediately called a team meeting and told them the story. I was proud of them and I told them all they had to do now was to just keep doing what they were doing – and that the other coach needed an inning to be ready for us to make outs and so we were gonna let the runner have it THIS INNING – but that was it.

We agreed, and the other coach was fine with playing outs after that. BUT ... it's a really good idea to check in with the other coach right before a game and make sure: "Are we good with pulling runners off the bases if we get an OUT."

Story: The best hug

This isn't a Tee Ball story but the one that caused me to be a coach, so I have to include it. In 1998 I was asked by a friend of mine to be an assistant to a Class AA team (ages 8-10). I agreed. The team had no pitchers and it was kid-pitch and I wasn't involved in the draft. I had no clue how to teach pitching, and neither did my friend the other coach. We lost every game.

We got a little better during the season, though, and it was a close loss in the playoffs to the first-place team, so there was some hope there.

During the season one kid climbed a tree during practice. I suddenly couldn't find him and then saw him way up in this tree. I got him to come down. I told him if he did it again I would make sure he would be thrown off the team. I said, "We have lost every game so far, and we are going to lose every game after this, and the last thing we need is a kid who climbs trees during practice! I'm more than happy to ask the league to remove you from the team so you can go do something else."

That kid reformed himself – he never climbed another tree, and he seemed to work a little harder. At the end-of-season party I was worn out; all that losing had gotten to me and I wasn't sure if I would coach any more. But at this party that little tree-climbing kid came over to say goodbye to me and just jumped into my arms with the biggest of hugs.

I never forgot him and that hug, and there was no way I wouldn't coach after that. The next year they asked if I wanted to be a head coach and I said YES. When the times are tough, I often think about that kid and that hug and I hope something good like that happens to everyone who reads this.

CONCLUSION

3 Key Messages

Message #1: Use as many assistants as possible

Coaching is just not done well if there is only one head coach and a couple of assistant coaches.

This staffing "plan" is a time-honored tradition. Of course you need a coach in the dugout and you need a first base coach and a third base coach. Issue three hats and three shirts and you are done.

I got my start in coaching youth baseball when a friend of mine asked me to be an assistant. I was one of his two assistants. It was chaos, none of us knew what we were doing, and we lost all our games at the AA level (kid pitch in Little League).

Fast-forward 23 years to the autumn of 2021. Again I was an assistant to a new head coach. He bought into my suggestion to bring in everyone we could get. Every practice we always had at least four assistants and some practices we had five or six. No one cared who was the "official assistants."

In right field we would have two coaches running the ground ball to pitcher then throw to first. In center field we would have a coach throwing fly balls along with me working with some pitchers – usually two at a time. In left field we would set up three batting stations with whiffle balls – small whiffle balls and swiftsticks with, you guessed it, three more coaches.

In the infield, the head coach and an assistant could work on infield defense, pitchers throwing off a real mound, ground balls, and other skills.

Count up the number of assistants in this outline – it's not two. It's more like seven or eight. No one was bored. Players got a lot of *quality* repetitions.

Practicing poor mechanics does not help. Try to do all you can to make sure that players are practicing good mechanics.

Using all these assistants does take some planning. You can't just show up; you have to know who is going to be there. You have to nail down who will be where and when. It's some work, but the benefits are huge. Our final record was 12-1, and we won the

"Practice does not make perfect. Only perfect practice makes perfect."

~ Vince Lombardi

regular season title and the league championship. More important, though, at the end-of-season party, I asked who was going to play next year. We had 13 kids on the team and 12 of them immediately said YES and one was a little shaky ... I expect he will play, but even if he doesn't, I'll take a 92 percent retention rate any day!

Message #2: Fundamentals, Fundamentals, Fundamentals

Stick to the fundamentals! So many coaches immediately want to work on the finer points of the game. Cut-offs, double steals, turning the double play, defending the bunt. These are all downstream from this book. This book is really all about having a good experience at Tee Ball, coach pitch, and the first year of kid pitch. Most leagues, at least those with some smarts, ban bunting at early kid-pitch levels as it's just too much on the defense to deal with it.

So what should you focus on? For pitching, all you care about is the strike percentage. You want the number of strikes thrown by pitchers in games to be over 50 percent. To do that in games, the pitchers need to reach 60-70 percent in practice. They have to constantly work on throwing to a target with good solid mechanics, and every pitch has to use the same motion.

For hitting, putting the ball in play is all you care about. To do this the batter has to be confident, set up at the plate the same way every time, and stay aware of the strike zone. Swinging at balls over their heads is not good. They also have to be looking to hit the ball.

On defense, throwing to a target is the key. If kids can't hit a big target, they aren't going to hit the glove of a player who is ready to catch the ball. Throwing is a skill that has to be worked on constantly so that throws are straight and players have confidence when they throw that it will go where they want it to go.

By failing to prepare, you are preparing to fail.
~ Benjamin Franklin

Catching is next. Just catching a ball correctly so that it's not a surprise if the ball is caught takes numerous repetitions. "Catching" ground balls requires good footwork and balance and also numerous repetitions. All this defensive work has to be perfected in the presence of live runners, so the players can get used to the notion of performing the basic fundamentals under the pressure of a runner about to advance to a base.

Keeping your goals simple to just THROW, CATCH, PUT BALL IN PLAY, THROW STRIKES is easy enough for young players to follow, and they can then build confidence. Any player – a not just your superstars – can do this.

Message #3: Maximize your practice time. Teach life lessons by setting an example that preparation is the key.

If the only thing this book does is convince you that practice time is special, I will be happy. In today's world getting a bunch of kids and parents outside in half-decent weather is a magical couple of hours. Most coaches I know sort of relish the games, but practice is not viewed as a big opportunity to teach life lessons and to teach mechanics. Some coaches schedule scrimmages with other teams just to get more games in and skip practices. To me they are saying "I don't have anything else to teach so let's just play and kids will learn from playing."

There is a bit of truth in this, and kids do get better from playing, but why then do major league players take hundreds of practice swings off a batting tee every day? They are preparing, that's why! They are practicing so they can perform better in a game. And these are adults playing 162 games a year!

Every one of my best teams practiced more than teams at the same level that did not do so well. Some teams just didn't want to come to optional extra practices – I frequently ask the league scheduler for optional extra practices. For years, I almost felt like I was cheating that the league let me have a practice field an extra day of the week – I was thinking I was lucky that I knew the scheduler and could score a field because I was on the board of directors – my grand inside knowledge was helping me get extra fields! The truth is, most teams don't *ask for* extra fields, so it was no big deal to give me one. Some leagues don't have time for you to get an extra field – but you can be creative by using someone's yard or your own or even a park – you'd be amazed how much you can do on a spare field. Just throwing and catching – hitting whiffle balls or tennis balls. You don't always need a baseball field to cover important baseball mechanics.

Think about it as if you are in a classroom teaching. Before you walk in to the room, you make a plan for the class, you prepare the materials, and then the actual class is all ready to go.

Even if you don't have time for extra practices, if you are reading this book, you are a coach and/or parent who cares about getting better and helping the kids get better. This means that you can take some of the ideas in this book and use the practices to maximize good repetitions. When I see players just walk slowly from one station to another I always feel annoyed; I know they are wasting time that could be used for them to get better. And they are wasting a precious little amount of time – maybe 90 minutes maybe two hours a week. Teaching kids that *preparing is a good way to achieve success* is a great life lesson. I don't know too many people who are successful who do no preparation at all – in fact, many of them spend countless hours on preparation. So plan your practices, make sure they are all organized, and see to it that everyone gets the most out of practice. Think about what you want to achieve, and after each practice think about what you might improve.

If you are COMMITTED to teaching kids and helping them improve and showing them the way, they will get there, and they'll learn concepts and habits that will serve them well for the rest of their lives.

ABOUT THE AUTHOR

David Grossman has been coaching youth baseball since 1999 and before that he coached adult softball for 10 years. "Coaching youth baseball is far better," he says.

He's coached all levels of Youth Baseball — Tee Ball, A, AA, AAA, Majors, All-Stars and Travel. He has served on his Little League board of directors and was Tee Ball Commissioner (one year), Quartermaster (four years), and Director of Safety and Training (one year) for Reston Little League in Virginia. He lived in England for three years where he served as the Minors Commissioner for London Little League.

"I have taught Computer Science for the last 25 years," says Coach Grossman. "I started as a graduate teaching assistant at the University of Central Florida. After that I was an Adjunct Professor at Maryland, George Mason and George Washington. I taught full time from 1999-2012 at the Illinois Institute of Technology, and in 2021 I became a faculty affiliate at Georgetown University in Washington DC."

"I have some idea of what works and what doesn't," he adds. "That doesn't mean I am a specialist with little kids; I actually started coaching before I had kids, so I think that gives me some perspective." His two boys, Isaac and Joseph have played on teams coached by their dad from the first years they were eligible to play.

ACKNOWLEDGMENTS

I must thank Jim Goldstein first – he agreed to be an assistant on my first team back in 1999 and he helped coach my teams all the years through my three-year move to England in 2012. He shares my love of the game and was always a fine sounding board about coaching. He helped me refine practice plans and develop devices to make practice go better – I may be able to sketch a thing on paper, but Jim can actually build it.

He is now an umpire, and last year he was selected to be on the officiating crew for the Virginia State Championship.

Next I have to thank Dr. Paul Allen, who started coaching with me when I had his two boys on my oldest son's first Tee Ball team in 2009. Paul is a true student of the game and reviewed and rewrote many portions of a large manuscript I wrote on coaching. This book has really evolved from that work, still on our website at **CoachingYouthBaseball.com**

Mr. Ben Goldfarb provided detailed technical copy edits to that earlier manuscript, and any good paragraphs in this book probably evolved from his fine work.

Mr. Joseph Foley really created **CoachingYouthBaseball.com** when I started it in 2014. His work was critical to its becoming a reality.

Mr. David C. Roberts is one of my first mentors from my day job – starting back in the 1980s. He now runs a search engine optimization company at **WebMarketingAdvantage.com** and has helped me increase website traffic enormously in the last few years.

Finally, numerous coaches have helped me over time. The one I look up to the most is Coach "Pudge" Gjormand at Madison High School, the winner of two state championships. I have attended many of his clinics and I have been lucky enough to talk to him on several occasions and review practice plans that he likes for Little League. Special thanks certainly is due to him.

Also, thanks to all the players and coaches and assistant coaches who have played on my teams. I wouldn't be much of a coach if it wasn't for them.

Thanks also to Reston-Herndon Little League, as the league is marvelously run and has always been very supportive of all my efforts to help out our coaches.

Special thanks goes to my sister Wendy Kantor, who took literally thousands of photos at numerous practices I held this summer. Those photos were the key to this book; a coaching book without pictures just isn't so great.

Afterword

I have wanted to write a book on coaching since at least 2010. I did publish a PDF on my website in 2015 that is about 200 pages. Some coaches have bought it and told me it is helpful. I'll keep it online as it covers all levels and has quite a bit of detailed content.

Over time, though, I really wanted a book with LOTS more pictures that could be available on Amazon as well as my website. Special thanks to a group of players who came to some mock practices this past summer and enabled me to collect over 3,500 pictures. Even more thanks has to go to Kelly Andersson at Andersson Publishing as she dealt with me off and on over the last two years and worked hard to bring this project together.

Feel free to send me any questions at
coachgrossman@coachingyouthbaseball.com

I wish you all the best with coaching and I hope you end up having as much fun coaching as I do.

Coach David Grossman
February 2022

RECOMMENDED RESOURCES

coachingyouthbaseball.com

Coaches Checklist (before you leave the house)
bit.ly/345X8wd

Quick-Start Guides (some tips to get started with coaching)
coachingyouthbaseball.com/quick-start-guides-landing/

Videos by Coach Grossman

American Baseball Coaches Association. The Baseball Drill Book. Human Kinetics. ISBN-0-7360-5083-3. 2004.

American Sports Education Program. Coaching Youth Baseball, Second Edition. Human Kinetics. ISBN-0-87322-965-7. 1996.

Baker, D. and Mercer, J. and Bittinger, M. You Can Teach Hitting. Masters Press. ISBN 0-940279-73-8. 1993.

Bagonzi, J. and Alex Levin. The Act of Pithing: A Tutorial for All Levels by a Master Technician Detailed Every Aspect of Pitching. Pitching Professor Publications. ISBN 0977825000, 2006.

Bennett, B. 101 Pitching Drills. Sagamore Publishing Inc. ISBN 1-57167-318-0. 1999.

Burroughs, J. Little League Instructional Guide. Bonus Books Inc. ISBN 1-56625-009-9. 1994.

Cluck, B. Play Better Baseball: Winning Techniques and Strategies for Coaches and Players. Contemporary Books Inc. ISBN 0-8092-3922-1. 1994.

Gola, M. and Monteleone, J. The Louisville Slugger Complete Book of Hitting Faults and Fixes. Contemporary Books. ISBN 0-8092-9802-3. 2001.

Hahne R. and Snyder, B. NVBA Youth Coaching Manual: The Coaches Companion. DemandTech Publishing. 1999.

House, T. and Heil, G. and Johnson, S. The Art and Science of Pitching. Coaches Choice. ISBN 158518960X. 2006.

Johnson, R. and Rosenthal, J. Randy Johnson's Power Pitching. Three Rivers Press. ISBN 1-4000-4739-0. 2003.

Mazzone, L and Rosenthal, J. Pitch Like a Pro. St. Martin's Griffin. ISBN 0-312-19946-5. 1999.

McFarland, J. Coaching Pitchers. Leisure Press. ISBN 0-88011-368-5. 1990.

McIntosh, N. Managing Little League Baseball. Contemporary Books. ISBN-0-8092-5322-4. 1985.

Monteleone, J. Coaching the Little League Hitter. McGraw-Hill. ISBN 0-07-141791-5, 2004.

Ripken, C. and Ripken, B and Burke, L. Play Baseball the Ripken Way: The Complete Illustrated Guide to the Fundamentals. Random House. ISBN-1-4000-6122-9. 2004.

Ryan, N. and House, T. Nolan Ryan's Pitchers' Bible: The Ultimate Guide to Power, Precision, and Long-Term Performance. Simon & Shuster. ISBN 0-671-70581-4. 1991.

Seaver, T. and Lowenfish, L. The Art of Pitching. Harper Paperbacks. ISBN 068813226X. 1994.

Southworth, S. The Complete Book of Baseball Signs and Plays, 2nd Edition. Coaches Choice. ISBN 1-58518-155-2. 1999.

Tamborra, S. Complete Conditioning for Baseball. Human Kinetics. ISBN 978-0-7360-6243-5. 2008.

Voorhees, R. Coaching the Little League Pitcher: Teaching Young Players to Pitch with Skill and Confidence. Contemporary Books. ISBN 0-07-140806-1. 2003.

Wilkin, J. and Kemble, J. and Coutts, M. Maximizing Baseball Practice, Human Kinetics. ISBN-0-87322-430-2. 1995.

Williams, T. and Underwood, J. The Science of Hitting. Simon & Shuster. ISBN 0-671-62103-3. 1986.

Winfield, D. and Swenson, E. Complete Baseball Player. Avon Books. ISBN 0-380-75830-x. 1990.

Made in the USA
Middletown, DE
07 February 2022

60675388R00080